right be a civil wrong?

# Journey to Joy

# Journey to Joy

## Living the Christian Life
## Philippians

### David Ray Gutierrez

Copyright © 2010 by David Ray Gutierrez.

ISBN:       Hardcover        978-1-4535-9130-7
            Softcover        978-1-4535-9129-1
            Ebook            978-1-4535-9131-4

All rights reserved. No part of this book may be reproduced or transmitted in any form or by any means, electronic or mechanical, including photocopying, recording, or by any information storage and retrieval system, without permission in writing from the copyright owner.

This book was printed in the United States of America.

To order additional copies of this book, contact:
Xlibris Corporation
1-888-795-4274
www.Xlibris.com
Orders@Xlibris.com
88184

# Contents

Introduction ................................................................... 7

## The Journey of Conduct—Philippians 1

1. The Journey of Servitude ............................................... 17
2. The Journey of Confidence ............................................ 23
3. The Journey of Love ..................................................... 32
4. The Journey of Gratitude ............................................... 41
5. The Journey of Decision ................................................ 47
6. Conclusion .................................................................. 52

## The Journey of Character—Philippians 2

7. The Journey Through Selflessness .................................. 61
8. The Journey Through Humility ....................................... 70
9. The Journey Through Commitment ................................. 79
10. The Journey Through Loyalty ........................................ 88
11. The Journey Through Persistence .................................. 94
12. Conclusion ................................................................ 100

## The Journey of Consequence—Philippians 3

13. The Journey Through Rejoicing .................................... 105
14. The Journey Through Truth .......................................... 113
15. The Journey Through True Christianity pt. 1 .................. 121
16. The Journey Through True Christianity pt. 2 .................. 127
17. The Journey Through Living The Christian Life .............. 134
18. Conclusion ................................................................ 140

## The Journey of Influence—Philippians 4

19  The Journey of Faithfulness .......................................................... 147
20  The Journey of Single-Mindedness ............................................. 153
21  The Journey of Example ............................................................... 159
22  The Journey of Contentment ....................................................... 169
23  The Journey of Promise ............................................................... 176
24  Conclusion ..................................................................................... 182

Works Consulted ................................................................................. 189

# Introduction

We have just returned from Del Rio, Texas, a trip that takes us 13 hours each way. I must confess that I am not much for traveling. I am more content to stay at home. But when my daughter and her family moved to Del Rio, I knew I would be traveling a lot. Having grandkids has a way of changing your way of life.

The first time we traveled to Del Rio I did a little research to see where this city was and the best way to get there. I got on Google Earth and entered my address here in Tucson and my destination, which was Del Rio, Texas. Then the earth began to move and the various little icons began to appear.

As the earth came to its final position, there it was, take I-10 East past El Paso and keep on going. Take exit 285 South, turn left and take 90 East until you get into Del Rio. Not having been to Del Rio, we were constantly looking at the map to make sure we were on the right road and headed in the right direction. It seemed like it was taking forever to get there. As we got to the first turn off, a thought popped into my head. "I wonder if there's a shorter and easier way to get to Del Rio."

Isn't that just the way we are? Wanting a shorter and easier way? We often miss the joy of the trip because we want to get there quickly. We look for those shortcuts. When it comes to our spiritual growth, don't we do that as well? We look for those shortcuts. We struggle with the length of the journey and the time it takes to become what God created us to be. We often miss the beauty of the journey to spiritual growth when we look for those shortcuts.

I've discovered that spiritual growth is more than just a moment in time. It is a daily process that includes those times which are hard and difficult. Yet, there are times when the journey is really enjoyable and rewarding.

Paul never cut corners to his spiritual growth. His life, after his encounter with Jesus, was always headed in the right direction. For him, the journey was rewarding even though he felt the weight and the heat of persecution. In spite of all that, he didn't cut corners or look for a better or shorter way. Paul once said, "Brothers, I have always lived before God with a clear conscience" (Acts 23:1 NLT).

That, in a nut shell, is the secret to living a joyful life. It is the very thing that makes this journey we have embarked on a joy. This journey to a joyful Christian life requires that we strive to live with a clear conscience before God. As I look back, I see the times in my spiritual walk that I did not have a clear conscience before God. Sometimes my pride would lead me to do things that would soon lead to regret and that regret led me into discouragement and fear.

We must be careful, though, in how we approach this journey. It's a dangerous thing to think that as Christians nothing will ever affect us in a wrong way or lead us in the wrong direction. We have a tendency to forget that our adversary, the devil, knows our weaknesses and he knows how to trip us up. Don't think for a moment that just because you have Jesus in your heart you know how to defeat the devil on your own power. If you think that, you've already lost the battle.

One of the best ways to prevent us from cutting corners in our spiritual journey is to emulate Paul. Paul's whole perspective was to be like Jesus. That was his goal, to be like Jesus. He said "For me to live is Christ" (Phil. 1:21 NASB). Again he says, "Instead, we will lovingly follow the truth at all times—speaking truly, dealing truly, living truly—and so become more and more in every way like Christ" (Eph. 4:15 TLB).

Have you ever wanted to be like someone? Maybe as a youngster you thought of yourself as Batman, Superman, Luke Skywalker or some other kind of hero? You watched and learned their every move. You dressed like them, talked like them and even tried to eat the same things they ate. I think that's why I gave up being like Popeye. I didn't really have his muscles unless you can call a pimple on my biceps a muscle. Also, Popeye ate spinach and I just didn't care for that leafy stuff.

Growing up I always wanted to be just like Superman. I had the red cape, the red underwear (from my sister's drawer), the red socks for boots, of course, and the blue tights. I was the Man of Steel, at least in my mind. I had this illusion, that I could truly jump off a building and fly like him. Now, I didn't actually go to a building, but I did do something just as crazy. I stood at the edge of our pitched roof and thought about jumping off. Something inside of me, kept me from doing that. Talk about personality disorder. I am beginning to realize though, as the years continually pile up behind me, I am turning more into my mother than Superman. I find myself saying some of the things she used to say to me. As I look into the mirror I can see a lot of her in me.

I think that is what Paul came to see. The more he turned his life over to Christ, the more he let Jesus influence him, the more he could see Jesus in himself. One of my favorite passages is found in Corinthians where it says, "All of us! Nothing between us and God, our faces shining with the brightness of his face. And so we are transfigured much like the Messiah, our lives gradually becoming brighter and more beautiful as God enters our lives and we become like him" (2 Cor. 3:18 MSG).

Paul made a commitment to follow God's leading, God's direction for his life, the moment he gave his life to Christ. As Christians we need to have that same distinct direction we are following. Sad to say, though, most of us as Christians have lost our direction. We have become undisciplined in our walk and we're content to just go through the motions. Without direction we stand a good chance to fail in our Christian walk or to minimize the power and the potential that this life has. Why? I believe it's because we have moved so far from the understanding of what the Christian life is. We say we are Christians but what does that mean? How do we show the world that we are truly different rather than indifferent? To be a Christian means what?

My friend Larry and I were headed to Globe, Arizona early last year to meet with my daughter's high school class. She had asked Larry if he would teach astronomy for the semester. Larry is working on his PhD in astronomy or was it astrology? I never can get those two right. Anyway, he volunteered to lead this part of my daughter's class. As we were traveling to Globe he entered the directions to the school into his GPS. Have you ever noticed how annoying these things can really be when you travel? This voice constantly reminds you what street or road you are passing.

As we got into town, I told him that my daughter said that if we stayed on this one street we would run into the school. But Larry being Larry, said no that his GPS told him to turn left and then turn right. So we listened to this machine and guess what? We ended up at a dead end. Go figure! After arguing for a few minutes, like some old married couple, we followed my daughter's instructions and we ran right into the school.

I've come to the conclusion that these machines aren't always right. When it concerns our spiritual life there is a strong possibility that, neither are we. When we choose our own way, when we depend on our own GPS (getting pridefully stupid), we can end up at a dead end. Even worse, we end up frustrated, empty and wondering. Listen, don't beat yourself up. If you've read God's Word, you've read about Abraham, Moses, David, Peter, Jonah and even the great Apostle Paul before his conversion. All of these guys did something pridefully stupid.

You remember the story of Abraham? God told him to leave the land of Ur and head out to a new place. He is going to a place (which, by the way, he has no real idea where he is going) and somewhere along the journey he stops trusting God and lies in order to save his neck. Abraham's lie and his lack of trust or faith brought about God's anger towards Pharaoh and his people (Gen. 12:10-20 NLT).

Moses, who had been instructed to lead the Israelites to the promise land, also changed his course. When he grew tired and angry with the people Moses did the exact opposite of what God told him to do. Moses didn't trust God enough to speak to the rock. Instead he decided that he was going to strike it and because of that God prevented him from entering the promise land (Num. 20).

How about David, the man after God's own heart? Here was this mighty king leading his army in battle. But one day he decided to go in a different direction. King David decided that he would stay in the palace and have a much deserved rest. Unfortunately, that decision led him to commit adultery, murder, and brought disgrace upon God's people (2 Sam. 11-12). David would later repent of his actions, but the damage had already been done.

How about Jonah? Now I know you know this story. God calls Jonah to go to Nineveh and preach, but instead Jonah chartered a different cruise and got into a whale of a mess (sorry, bad joke). He had an opportunity to speak the Word of God to a godless nation and he freaked out and took off in a different direction. Afterwards, after listening to God he went to Nineveh and preached and that city got saved. But Jonah felt cheated. God hadn't done what he thought should have been done. He really felt that God had let him down.

Then there is Peter who, after the crucifixion of Jesus, decided he was going to go his own direction and he went out to fish. It didn't matter that he had just spent three years with Jesus. It didn't matter that he had seen thousands fed, miracles displayed and that he had walked on water. He was going to choose his direction now. He was going fishing. Actually, the New Testament says he went back to his old line of work. He not only changed his direction and gave up the ministry but he took with him others as well (John 21).

Even Paul (Saul before his conversion), who thought he was doing God's work, was brought to his knees by God on the road to Damascus. Here was a man highly educated in the Jewish faith. Here was a man that held a high position and even commanded the respect of the religious leaders and still he couldn't see that he was going in the wrong direction. So God blinded him, humbled him, and set him on the right course.

God had to intervene in the lives of these men before the situation got real ugly. His Word and greatness were at stake so God caused certain situations to take place. Not only was He watching out for His great name, He was watching out for the lives of these people. He could have let them go on to destruction, but He had greater plans for them. So, if you think God doesn't care about the direction you are going, you might want to rethink that.

Choosing our own direction may seem like the right thing to do, but in the end we find ourselves empty, hopeless and uncertain about our lives. God says to us, "'if you look for me wholeheartedly, you will find me. I will be found by you,' says the Lord. 'I will end your captivity and restore your fortunes. I will gather you out of the nations where I sent you and will bring you home again to your own land'" (Jer. 29:13-14 NLT).

In this journey of the Christian faith we actually need a GPS to get us through the rough roads, those high mountains and the deep valleys of life. I am firmly convinced that as believers we will never find real joy without this GPS. The GPS I'm talking about is one that actually speaks to us personally in a soft, gentle voice, gives guidance and let's us know that we may be headed in a wrong direction. That GPS is *God's Powerful Spirit*. Or you could say it is *God's Personal Spirit*. "But when He, the Spirit of truth, comes, He will guide you into all the truth; for He will not speak on His own initiative, but whatever He hears, He will speak; and He will disclose to you what is to come" (John. 16:13 NASB).

To journey in the right direction is to understand what it means to be a Christian and how to live that Christian life. I am discovering that there is a huge misconception about this Christian life and the joy we can have while we journey through this life. What I have witnessed these last few months while visiting and preaching in different churches has led me to believe that the Christian life has become one of form without substance. We call ourselves Christian but our lives and actions say otherwise. Paul's letter to the Philippians lays the foundation for true Christianity. His hopes and desires is that this letter would make it clear what the Christian walk is all about and the joy that comes from knowing how to live it.

I have lived my Christian life making decisions that benefitted me rather than letting the Lord lead and guide. However, in the last few years God has given me an opportunity to learn and listen to His direction and the meaning of really living the Christian life. I am grateful for the time He has given me to be able to put into print what He has been teaching me. The writer of this Proverb says, "If you listen to advice and are willing to learn, one day you will be wise" (Prov. 19:20 TEV).

I pray that as you read through this book you will discover something new and fresh about being a Christian and the joy you can have each day regardless of the circumstances facing you. I wonder if you wouldn't mind traveling with me, or better yet taking this journey where you can find God's fulfilling direction. I want to encourage you to come with me on this journey to joy.

Before we begin this journey, I want to make sure you know what this is all about. Making this kind of journey without the power or purpose behind it, well, will leave you frustrated. You need this GPS I have been talking about, which is Jesus Christ. The Bible says that unless *you confess Jesus as Lord*, unless you are willing to admit that you have been going in the wrong direction, this journey will be pointless. It also says that unless *you believe in your heart that God raised Him from the dead*, or unless you accept the fact that Jesus is the only way, you cannot really have the power to get through this journey.

So my question to you is do you have this relationship with Jesus? Have you ever asked Him into your life? Have you admitted to Him that you have been going in the wrong direction and that you need His forgiveness? It's really very simple. Right where you're sitting, just close your eyes or at least bow your head and just say this;

"Dear God, I know You know the life I have been living. I am not really proud of what I have done or the way I have been living. Right now would You forgive me of my sin as I invite You into my heart? I am asking this in Your Son's name, Jesus Christ. Amen"

The rest of the passage says, "For with the heart a person believes, resulting in righteousness, and with the mouth he confesses, resulting in salvation. For the Scripture says, 'Whoever believes in Him will not be disappointed'" (Rom. 10:9-11 NASB).

Your journey to joy begins the moment Christ enters your heart. Notice he says that you will not be disappointed. Listen, I am not going to tell you that everything in this journey is going to be easy. I know that is what a lot of well meaning Christian preachers and teachers will have you believe. That is not what Paul is saying here. He of all people knows that this life will have many mountain and valley experiences. What he is saying to you is that regardless of what you may be going through, God will always, always have His loving arms around you. You will never be alone nor will you ever be dissatisfied. Deuteronomy 31:6 says, "Be strong and of good courage . . . for the Lord your God, He is the One who goes with you. He will not leave you nor forsake you" (NKJV). Now let's take a trip.

# The Journey of Conduct

## Philippians 1

# 1

# The Journey of Servitude
# Philippians 1:1-5

Gayla and I have been in the ministry for a little over thirty years. We've just concluded an interim with the Father's Heart Church. About three years ago a young man and his wife, who had two young autistic boys, came to Tucson to begin a new work. God impressed upon their hearts to begin a ministry where families dealing with autistic children could find fellowship and support. The couple also saw a need and provided a place where these children could get an education.

After a few years this young man and his wife were called to a new place of service. Because of my relationship with them and their church, they called us to serve as their interim while they considered a new pastor for their ministry. We accepted the invitation and served them for seven months. It was a wonderful experience.

Previous to this, we committed ourselves for three years to help restart a local Brethren church in the Tucson community. I really felt God impressing upon my heart to serve there. After meeting with the Senior Pastor of the church and the District Officer of this denomination we felt this was the place where God was leading us to serve.

As Southern Baptist we were somewhat concerned about serving in another denomination. It was not exactly the direction I had in mind for our lives. But God convicted my heart about this. He showed me that this was a great opportunity to serve for the Gospel's sake and help a ministry grow rather than see another church close its doors.

Now we find ourselves looking for another opportunity to serve. I have served as a senior pastor and as an associate pastor for Southern Baptist churches. I was also a pastor to college students for five years. I even spent a few years as a contemporary Christian singer and songwriter. Last but not least, I have served as a worship leader.

For almost a year now I have been sending out resumes to churches around the country looking for the next place God would have us serve. I've received many kind letters from the churches I have applied to. It's funny how they all seem to say the same thing, "Dear Rev. Gutierrez, we are grateful you have taken an interest in our ministry. But at this time we have decided to go in a different direction." What does going in a different direction mean?

God does not always lead us in the same direction when it concerns His Word and work. At times He may lead us through a period of rest or to serve in other ways. In this last year, we've had several opportunities to serve other churches in different ways during our search for God's next assignment. We've helped new church starts by providing the music for their worship. We have served as worship leaders for worship pastors going on vacations. I have been traveling to some extent preaching in pulpits across the state and in revivals as the music evangelist.

Now, I've said all of this because sometimes I get the impression from other Christians that they think we have to have some position in the church to be servants. Servitude does not always have to include position, nor a monetary reward. It could be that God wants us to serve Him regardless of the position or the recognition. He wants our hearts not just our abilities.

One of the best examples of servitude is Nehemiah, a godly man serving in a position that many today would consider degrading or beneath them. Nehemiah was a cupbearer or, a better way of saying it, he was a servant of the king. His service to the king was one of great importance. The cupbearer was responsible for serving wine at the king's table and protecting the king from being poisoned. The cupbearer was often taken into the king's confidence and had great influence on the king's decisions (Neh. 1 & 2 NASB).

As you read through Nehemiah's book you will discover that God used him to do an even greater work. He became the one that led the children of God to rebuild the Jerusalem walls. Here was a servant who became a leader. Why? Because Nehemiah's conduct was one of faithfulness. His character was impeccable. He was a man that knew and understood the consequences of his life's actions and decisions. He was a man of great influence. But what made Nehemiah the man that he was? His prayer at the beginning of his book reveals why he was who he was. "I beseech Thee, O LORD God of heaven, the great and awesome God . . . let Thine ear now be attentive and Thine eyes open to hear the prayer of Thy servant . . . " (Neh.1:5-6 NASB77). He saw himself not as a servant of the earthly king, but as the servant of the God of heaven.

That is why I like what Paul had to say at the beginning of this letter to the Philippians, "Paul and Timothy, servants of Christ Jesus, to all the saints in Christ Jesus at Philippi, together with the overseers and deacons: Grace and peace to you from God our Father and the Lord Jesus Christ. I thank my God every time I remember you. In all my prayers for all of you, I always pray with joy because of your partnership in the gospel from the first day until now . . . . " (Phil. 1:1-5 NIV).

Paul uses several descriptive words in the first few verses of this letter. He says they were, servants, saints, overseers, deacons and partners. Nothing could be clearer as to what Paul believed a Christian was and what a Christian did. The word "servant" in the Greek means "slave." It conveys the meaning or the idea of someone who willingly submits himself to the authority and wishes of another. The word "saint" carries the idea of "one that is set apart for a particular purpose." The "overseers and deacons" are described as leaders that serve the church.

Notice that Paul does not identify himself as an Apostle but as a servant along with these others. It is inclusive of all believers whether we are leaders or not. Servitude is one of the characteristics of true believers. This is where I believe we must begin if our journey to joy is to be successful. We are servants of God and we are called to serve one another. "As each one has received a gift, use it to serve one another as good stewards of God's varied grace" (1 Pet. 4:10 NAB).

Several thoughts come to mind as we read this passage. First, our journey will always lead us through *servitude*. From the pastor to the person sitting in the pew, all are servants. But not just any servant. We are servants of the most High God, servants of the Lord Jesus Christ. No title can ever compare to that of *servant of the Lord*. You and I cannot claim any special position in God's presence or in this world. We are here to serve—serve God and serve people.

In our daily lives we should always be aware of the fact that we are to *serve one another*. It begins with Jesus and then others. We must be the servants of God in our homes. We are to be servants to our neighbors and also in the communities we live and socialize in. We are also called to be servants in other communities as well.

In the Apostle's mind he saw himself as just that, a servant. Paul never set himself above others. In his ministry his only purpose was to please God and serve others. I can't think of a single passage where Paul demands that others serve him. As a matter of fact, Paul would basically do whatever he could to provide for his needs. He never let his burden become someone else's burden.

I am amazed at how some Christian leaders seem to think that God has placed them in some ministry to be served. I've met several pastors who are more concerned about money than they are about missions. They dress flashy, drive fancy cars, eat at fine restaurants and strut their stuff like some proud rooster in a hen house. Servitude is not some lowly position for the less educated or fortunate. Servitude is a privilege. To be called to serve God is one of the most awesome callings anyone can have. That is why Paul is a great character to emulate. He never considered his service to be degrading, but rewarding.

He says: "For God, whom I serve in my spirit in the preaching of the gospel of His Son, is my witness as to how unceasingly I make mention of you, always in my prayers making request, if perhaps now at last by the will of God I may succeed in coming to you. For I long to see you so that I may impart some spiritual gift to you, that you may be established; that is, that I may be encouraged together with you while among you, each of us by the other's faith, both yours and mine. I do not want you to be unaware, brethren, that often I have planned to come to you (and have been prevented so far) so that I may obtain some fruit among you also, even as among the rest of the Gentiles." (Rom. 1:9-13 NASB).

At the beginning of this letter to the Philippians Paul included all of the leadership he was writing to. Christian service is not for certain people. The service of the Kingdom is not for pastors only. Service is for all of the believers of the church whether they are paid staff or volunteers. Paul told the Christians at Ephesus, "Serve wholeheartedly, as if you were serving the Lord, not men" (Eph. 6:7 NIV).

As Christians we have been called to serve and not be served. Jesus said, "But many who are first will be last, and many who are last will be first." Then in the Gospel of John, Jesus says, "Whoever serves me must follow me; and where I am, my servant also will be. My Father will honor the one who serves me" (Matt. 19:30 NIV; John 12:26 NIV).

So this journey of joy we are taking has to go through the willingness of being or becoming a servant. We are called to serve. Now, this isn't always easy especially in church ministry. Sometimes, when we faithfully serve in the church, people don't always show their gratitude. We may not get highlighted in the church newsletter, but we are still called to serve. That is never an option. It comes as needs increase, and in the church needs are always increasing as the church is growing.

Look at what was taking place as the church began to grow. In Acts 6:1-4 it says, "Now at this time while the disciples were increasing in number, a complaint arose on the part of the Hellenistic Jews against the native Hebrews, because their widows were being overlooked in the daily serving of food . . . " The Apostles had to appoint others to help provide the service needed for this growing community of believers. Pastors and other leaders are not responsible for all the ministry or service. It requires the whole community of believers and that includes you and me.

It doesn't end there, nor does it ever go unnoticed by God. Listen to what Paul tells us again, "Grace and peace to you from God our Father and the Lord Jesus Christ"(v.2). What is grace? Well, grace is unmerited favor, something that is unearned and undeserved. But it also carries the idea of "blessing" and "thankfulness." Think with me for a moment. When we willingly serve, when we give of our time unselfishly, our money and our abilities, God blesses us. That is the second thing that we find here. *God always blesses His people* when they are faithful in their service.

God always sees our heart and knows our intent. When He sees us serving Him unselfishly, He willingly blesses us. He gives back to us in different ways. I like that. I like the fact that God is always willing to give back to us when we sacrificially serve Him and others. Paul tells Timothy, "Warn the rich people of this world not to be proud or to trust in wealth that is easily lost. Tell them to have faith in God, who is rich and blesses us with everything we need to enjoy life" (1 Tim. 6:17 CEV).

Here is another way to look at this. The word "grace" also carries with it the idea of "thankfulness." Just imagine that all of your work goes unnoticed by the people you serve. That would get very discouraging don't you think? I know I would be discouraged by it. But let's just suppose while that may be truer than we care to admit, God is thanking us for our service. *He is thanking us by blessing us*. How cool would that be? In the words of my four-year-old granddaughter, Breya, "That is awesome!" When I think about that, well, this journey of joy through servitude is really not that bad. God, who is loving and gracious and ever-watchful, gives to us and is thankful for what we are doing. That is just simply awesome!

Finally, I want to call your attention to the word "peace." This word has a particular meaning and Paul uses it here for a very special reason. The word "peace" here means "an attitude of heart." In a sense, it is "tranquility of heart." When we serve willingly and unselfishly, God blesses us and thanks us. By resting in that truth, we enter into the realm of "calm assurance." No matter what may be happening around us or even to us, if we are in the center of God's purpose for our lives, then and only then, can we achieve "calm assurance" or as the hymn writer says, "blessed assurance."

Are we doing what we are called to do? Let's make this personal. Are you doing what you were called to do? This week were you serving or were you silent? As Christians we are called to serve as partners in ministry. That's what Paul meant when he said "because of your partnership in the gospel" (v.5). He saw the Philippian Christians as partners in the faith. Churches do not grow because of buildings, but because of *partnering believers* in the Gospel. To have joy in our hearts and in our lives we need to become serving partners in the faith. Each one has a gift and the responsibility to employ that gift within the community of believers.

One of the gifts we can implement in our lives, right now, is the ministry of prayer. Our joy can be magnified when we serve others through prayer for one another. Paul prayed for these believers daily. He said "I thank my God every time I remember you. In all my prayers for all of you, I always pray with joy" (vs. 3-4). We all need that in our lives. We all need to be prayer warriors for one another and have other people praying for us. Paul tells the Ephesian Christians, "In the same way, prayer is essential in this ongoing warfare. Pray hard and long. Pray for your brothers and sisters. Keep your eyes open. Keep each other's spirits up so that no one falls behind or drops out" (Eph. 6:18 MSG).

# 2

# The Journey Of Confidence
# Philippians 1:6

Nothing can shatter our confidence like some unexpected, bad news. Here we are living life and doing things and never really thinking that tomorrow may be different. The Bible tells us, "How do you know what your life will be like tomorrow? Your life is like the morning fog—it's here a little while, then it's gone" (James 4:14 NLT).

Last year while on a regular visit, my doctor noticed a mole that didn't seem right to her. She suggested I see a dermatologist to have it checked out. I did as she asked. The dermatologist checked all my moles, and he, too, wanted to take a closer look at one in particular. As he pulled out his little mole spy glass, he noticed something in that mole didn't look right. He had me lie down and he proceeded to remove that one mole. The doctor said he would send it to the lab to be analyzed. Two days later, while sitting in my office at the church, the doctor called and told me to make an appointment at the Cancer Center. I had melanoma.

Now, I didn't know exactly what that meant. When I arrived at home that afternoon, I received a call from the Cancer Center. The young lady on the phone told me that the dermatologist had called her and that she had already scheduled me for a meeting with the cancer doctor in the next two weeks.

By this time I was really getting concerned. I asked her what my chances were and she said if I let it go any longer it could prove fatal. Wow! Talk about being knocked to the floor. I told her that the appointment she had set up would not be possible. We had already scheduled a family vacation in San Diego. The nurse said that was okay. They would meet with me when I returned.

I cannot express to you all my uncertainties and questions in life. My family has a history of cancer and I had that feeling I would not be as lucky. All the time we were in San Diego, I couldn't help but think about my future. Going to Sea World and all the other attractions we had scheduled couldn't take my mind off what was going to happen to me when I returned.

The day of my appointment arrived and my wife, Gayla, met me at the Cancer Center. I really hate waiting. I hate waiting in a doctor's office even more. When we met the doctor, he had me lie on the table while he and his assistant looked the area over. He then proceeded to let me know my chances and how the procedure works. He was very patient and compassionate. I just didn't really hear much of what he was saying except the word cancer.

Surgery was not a yes or no option, it had to be done. I have had only had one surgery in my life and I don't remember much of it. I was only seven at the time I entered the hospital for some major surgery. I still don't know how to describe it. I learned later in life that for a brief moment I had died on that table. Now I was facing that possibility again and the one thing I kept thinking was "Am I ready?"

After all the surgical participants had their say, I lay there thinking, "What is heaven like?" "Will I wake up to find that something else has gone wrong?" "Why am I even going through this?" "Is it because of all the wrong choices I made along this journey?" In the midst of all of this, I overlooked one important thing, my relationship with the Lord.

I don't care how certain you are about your Christian walk, when faced with a major unexpected crisis, sometimes God can get left out of the equation. That's what I did this time. The surgery was a success, but I had to wait two more weeks to find out that I wouldn't need any more treatment. The doctor was very positive and assured me that he had done this procedure with a 95% success rate. "Great", I thought, "I'll take that."

Confidence is something a lot of us have trouble with. Here we are on this journey through life and all of a sudden a speed bump in the road makes us slow down or stop completely. Once that happens, it's really difficult to get going again.

A lot of things can rattle our confidence along this journey. It could be a miserable or abusive home life. It could be a broken marriage or relationship. It could be serious financial matters that weigh heavily on our hearts or an ongoing health issue. When we hit that bump, watch out! It's really hard to get up and get going again after a major setback.

I am reminded of a story in Matthew chapter eight. It's really a unique story. Jesus is just finishing His message to the people. As He is coming down from the mount with all sort of people following him, a man with leprosy falls before him and pleads his case. Notice what the passage says, "When he came down from the mountainside, large crowds followed him. A man with leprosy came and knelt before him and said, 'Lord, if you are willing, you can make me clean'" (Matt. 8:1-2 NIV). As I read that, it made me think about how this man's life was so different from how it began. I'm certain it didn't begin with this disease. This was something that probably happened unexpectedly.

Prior to being overcome by this leprosy, he probably had a job and a family, though the Bible doesn't tell us much about him. But I would imagine that when he caught leprosy no one wanted to be around him. History tells us that in those days people with leprosy had to live outside of the city and had to call out when they entered a populated area, "Unclean, Unclean." Can you imagine if this had been you? Would you be really confident about your life if you had to announce your illness? No, you wouldn't and neither would I and neither was he. He had a shattered confidence and only one person could do something about it, or at least that is what he'd hope for.

What is, *confidence*, anyway? We've been talking about it and if we are to obtain it on our journey, then what is it? Well, the dictionary defines it this way; (1) the belief that one can have faith in or rely on someone or something; (2) self-assurance arising from an appreciation of one's abilities. I want to use Paul and this leprous man to illustrate these two definitions.

I find it interesting that Paul has an unwavering confidence in the midst of great uncertainty. Paul says, "I am confident of this very thing, that He who began a good work in you will complete it" (Phil.1:6 NASB). Paul wasn't dealing with some serious illness, though he certainly knew the hardships of physical pain. Paul was separated from those he loved and was unable to do the things he had been doing. Yet, as we see in verse six he has this unheard of confidence. Why? Well, hold on, I am going to come back to this in a moment.

Let's look at the man with leprosy. Here he is, and, you've got to love this guy, he'd had enough of this isolation and this painful, annoying disease. It is said that this disease was so cruel that it would literally cause a person's body to deform to the point where they didn't look human. It robbed them of their dignity and their acceptance in the community. So when he comes to Jesus, he didn't come with the presumption that Jesus would or could do anything for him. He was just desperate for something to happen. His own words reveal the fact that he had lost all confidence, "If You are willing?"

A lot of us feel the way this leprous man felt. We may not have this disease, but our sin makes us feel the same way. I am not so foolish to think that on this journey we won't make mistakes or decide to chart our own course. Every Christian has tried to outguess God or tried to run ahead of Him, only to find themselves fearful and ashamed.

Like this leprous man, we find ourselves kneeling before Jesus saying, "If You are willing." We don't have any confidence or assurance that He will take us back. We feel that way because we have failed. We feel He no longer has any use for us. Listen, I know how that feels. When we fail, some in the Christian community ignore us and some exclude us. Nothing can make us feel more like this leprous man than unforgiving Christians who won't have anything to do with us.

Paul finds himself as well facing an unwelcome situation. Here he had been preaching and teaching and all of a sudden he finds himself in prison simply because of his faith. Some sought to embarrass Paul and some probably ridiculed him because he was in prison. I'm sure that many were frightened to come close to him for fear they might be thrown into prison as well. Day in and day out he was never alone. He always had two guards on either side. You can bet they were not the gentle kind either. Can you imagine being chained to these tough guys day after day, hearing them swear and making fun of you? Paul was not in the best of situations.

Yet, I find it really amazing, almost beyond comprehension, that he could still say, "I am confident of this very thing, that He who began a good work in you will complete it" (1:6). This is really a description of the first definition found in the dictionary, "the belief that one can have faith in or rely on someone or something." Listen, Paul's confidence was anchored to a person. Paul didn't depend on his abilities or courage to see him through. He didn't place his confidence on the people around him who are praying for him either. He certainly didn't place his confidence on the present-day government to find him innocent of any crimes. He says he placed his confidence on this very thing, "He who began a good work." It is this "He" in whom he has all his confidence.

Let's return to the man with leprosy. Here is this man who probably was really confidant about who he was and what he was able to do before his illness. He probably had people who admired him and the work he had accomplished. He had friends and family all around him. Life was good and he was happy.

That is where a lot of us are today. We are confident in life because we have our health or a good job, a wonderful family and lots of friends. But what if all those things are taken away, what then? What are we anchored to? This is where this man with leprosy probably took the wrong direction in life. He had placed his confidence on himself and his abilities and on those around him. That is a good example of the second definition of confidence, "self-assurance arising from an appreciation of one's abilities." I am stating this second definition in a negative way simply because most of us begin with ourselves and with our abilities.

But look at what Paul says again, "I am confident that **HE WHO BEGAN** a good work." Paul is looking at life from a different perspective. There is no way his position at this particular moment is going to get any better. In fact it will get a lot worse. He is in prison and facing death and yet his confidence is not in the person he is. He doesn't anchor his confidence in himself. A lot of Christians do the exact opposite of Paul. They anchor their whole basis for the Christian life on who they are. They believe, like so many of us, that even though their lives were totally wretched, when God came and saved them, well, He got a pretty good deal. So, then we go on thinking that we are special. We anchor ourselves on that belief and we play out our Christian walk based on that kind of thinking.

I know what you are thinking, "That's not what I have done!" You may have or may not have done that. I know that many times I have charted the wrong course simply because I was so confident about who I was that I thought I didn't really need God to lead and guide me. I found, that in those times when I went my own way, when I used my own GPS (getting pridefully stupid), my confidence in my spiritual life wavered. So it doesn't surprise me that this leprous man had no confidence in what Jesus was able to do. He had been let down by his health, his friends and family and even his community. Could Jesus really do what he longed to have done?

That is exactly where I was. When faced with an unexpected and unwanted situation, my confidence in who I was, what I was doing and where I was going began to diminish. I felt like this poor leprous man saying the same thing, "If You are willing You can make me clean or whole again." Our confidence can only come when we are anchored to Jesus Christ. Jesus said, "Verily, verily, I say unto thee, Except a man be born again, he cannot see the kingdom of God" (John 3:3 KJV). So it begins by accepting Jesus and placing our trust in Him. God helps us see our lives and where they are headed when we're in control. But He will also help us see where our lives could be headed if we put Him in control. So we all need His grace, His offer of freedom.

Why? Because the Bible tells us, "For all have sinned, and come short of the glory of God" (Rom. 3:23 KJV). It doesn't say some have sinned or only a few have sinned, but all have sinned and that means you and me. "Jesus said . . . 'I am the way, the truth, and the life. No one comes to the Father except through Me.'" (John 14:6 NKJV).

So many times we find ourselves trying to build our own bridges to God. We decide that the only way to prove that we are truly spiritual is, maybe, start a church. Or we think in order to be spiritual we need to get involved in some ministry in the church. Or we think that by giving a generous amount of money to missions or some project we can add to our spirituality.

All of those things are good, but they cannot add to or make us spiritual. Paul says he is confident in God. Now the word "confident" can also mean "convinced." Many of us are convinced that we can chart our own course. Remember, Jonah thought he could. Or Moses or even Paul? We convince ourselves by doing the things we want and by charting the journey we want to take. But Jesus says, "Enter through the narrow gate" (Matt. 7:13 NAB). In other words, this gate, this road, this journey that leads to spiritual maturity can only be possible when we leave all our baggage, our pride and arrogance at the narrow gate or, to say it a different way, at the foot of the cross.

Now, what I am saying is that we have to be convinced that God is the One who is working in our lives. We have to have this unwavering confidence that HE IS THE ONE WHO HAS BEGUN THE WORK, in our lives. Why? Because when I am convinced that He is working in me, I am confident. When He is the One leading me, I gain confidence. When I am doing what He has called me to do, then and only then, do I experience this unwavering confidence that Paul had.

Once we have taken that step of faith we need to continue in that pathway. Many people stop here. They get their fire insurance and then go out and live recklessly. Jesus said in order to really grow as a Christian we not only have to accept Him and trust in Him, but we also have to abide in Him. "Abide in Me, and I in you. As the branch cannot bear fruit of itself, unless it abides in the vine, neither can you, unless you abide in Me. I am the vine, you are the branches. He who abides in Me, and I in him, bears much fruit; for without Me you can do nothing" (John 15:4-5 NKJV).

Then, we not only accept and abide, but we also seek to apply. Paul said, "Study to show thyself approved unto God, a workman that needeth not to be ashamed, rightly dividing the word of truth" (2 Tim.2:15 KJV). We must act on or apply what we learn. If I accept training manuals for flying a plane and abide by the rules set forth for pilots, but never put it into practice what good does it do me? I have the information and the tools, but no experience. Likewise, I need to apply what I learn in God's Word if my Christian life is going to be fruitful.

"Always remember what is written in the Book of the Teachings. Study it day and night to be sure to obey everything that is written there. If you do this, you will be wise and successful in everything" (Joshua 1:8 NCV).

"For Ezra had set his heart to study the law of the Lord and to practice it, and to teach His statutes and ordinances in Israel" (Ezra 7:10 NASB).

This journey to joy must not only go through servitude, but it must also have an unshakeable confidence. We have to have confidence in Him that He is continuing the work in us as we go through this journey. I am not talking about confidence in what we can do, but in recognizing what God can do and is doing. That is where Paul drew his confidence.

Now, Paul tells us that God has begun a good work in each of us. As a Christian, as a believer, our salvation is totally dependent on what God is able to do. We cannot save ourselves. We cannot do enough good works to get us into heaven. Our gifts and talents are not enough to earn us salvation. God is the author of our faith and salvation. Hebrews 12:2 says, "Let us fix our eyes on Jesus, the author and perfecter of our faith . . . " Salvation never begins with us.

Also, our salvation is not dependent on our abilities. This is where a lot of well-meaning Christians get on the wrong road. They think that just because they can grow a ministry or have a TV ministry every week, spend thousands and thousands of dollars on buildings and theme parks that they are really spiritual. Somehow they are safe and secure in the belief that God must really be proud of them.

Paul says, "No!" The way to confidence is through understanding that God is the One who starts and finishes what He desires. God in His infinite wisdom knows where and when to begin a good work. I could be the greatest preacher in the world, but if I set out to plant a church and God is not in it then it will fail. God begins and I allow Him to lead. He plants and I water. He decides and I obey.

The man with leprosy was healed, not because he was special or had anything to offer, but because he placed his confidence in what Jesus could do. Jesus had compassion on Him. Jesus stretched out His hand and touched him, saying, "I am willing; be cleansed. Immediately his leprosy was cleansed" (Matt. 8:3 NASB). It was all Jesus. This man had nothing to do with his cleansing. His only part was to come and admit that he needed something greater than himself. He needed Jesus.

The response from Jesus was really amazing here. He never asked this guy to do anything before He healed him. He never demanded that he recite the Ten Commandments nor does He question his motives in asking for healing. He simply said this, "I am willing."

You and I don't have to beg God for forgiveness. We don't have to light a certain number of candles or walk a certain number of miles before He listens to our request. He simply just forgives us. This leprous man had nothing to offer except himself just as he was. Not much of an offering, wouldn't you agree?

Yet, here is the love of God displayed ever so clearly, "He touched him." Wow! Don't do that, Jesus, he might be contagious or something! Isn't that how we approach people from the outside? We hold them at a distance hoping they don't accidently rub against us. If there is anything that I have learned these past thirty some years is that people want to be loved, they want to be forgiven and they want to be accepted.

Jesus reaches out and touches this guy. Can you imagine how the crowd reacted to that? I am sure they had made a very wide clearing for this guy. Why did Jesus even have to touch him? Couldn't He have just spoken a simple word of cleansing and this guy would be healed? I'm sure that Jesus could have spoken a word and everything would have been all right. But this man needed more than a word, he needed to know that he was loved. People don't care about the Jesus we talk about. They want to see this Jesus acted out in our lives. They want to see if what He has done in our lives really translates into genuine love and concern.

So dear friend, don't give up on life just because you made a few bad choices. God loves you and in this very moment He has His arms around you. I need that and I'm sure you do, too. Here is a promise you may want to hang onto, "He will complete it." Paul placed his confidence on the fact that in whatever God promises, whatever He starts, He will see it through. On this journey to joy we can have that assurance just like Paul. "He who began a good work in you will complete it until the day of Jesus Christ." When God begins a project, there is nothing that will prevent Him from completing it.

> "O Lord, I will honor and praise your name,
> for you are my God.
> You do such wonderful things!
> You planned them long ago,
> and now you have accomplished them."
> (Isaiah 25:1 NLT)

# 3

# The Journey Of Love
# Philippians 1:7-11

What is love? We hear it in songs and we see it played out in the movies and we even use this word to describe how we feel about something. Most of us are fond of saying we love peach cobbler or cheesecake. Or we love going to that mall or that dress shop. We love gardening or sitting and reading a book. It's funny how this word has been used in every way imaginable.

But what is love? The dictionary describes this word like this, (1) an intense feeling of deep affection. (2) a deep romantic or sexual attachment to someone. Now, if we were to use this word based on these definitions I would find it very hard to believe I could have deep romantic feelings for my garden or food or anything like that. It would be rather silly to have an on-going relationship with my peach cobbler or cheesecake.

I know it sounds stupid or silly, but we use this word many times in foolish and meaningless ways. We really don't have intense feelings of deep affection for things that simply cannot return that same intensity, right? I can love my guitar, but it cannot love me back.

So what is love? Well, the Bible defines love this way, "But God demonstrates His own love toward us, in that while we were yet sinners, Christ died for us" (Rom. 5:8 NASB). Love is placing a value on something that at one point has no value or is marred in some way. Paul goes on to say "while we were yet sinners." That means we were at one point against God or, as the Bible puts it, enemies of God.

Romans 3 says, "No one is righteous— not even one. No one is truly wise; no one is seeking God. All have turned away; all have become useless. No one does good, not a single one" (vs.10-12 NLT). Nothing you and I could do can ever bring us to a relationship with God. We weren't even looking for God. Like most people, we were out to live life on our terms. In John 3:16 it says, "For God so loved the world **THAT HE GAVE** His only begotten son, that whosoever believes in Him would not perish but have life everlasting."

God took the initiative to demonstrate His love even while we were still living life on our terms. He made a way for us to come to Him by sacrificing what was precious to Him, His Son. If you have children you know how precious they are. It would be very difficult to sacrifice them for any reason (though at times we have probably thought about it).

Listen, God doesn't love us because we are special people or because we are fun to be with. He didn't love me because He liked the way I could sing or the way I could preach. But that is what a lot of Christians think, they think God loved them and saved them because they were very special people. "Look God, you really got something here!" No, God loves us not for who we are or what we are or what we can do. He loves us because of the value He places on the heart. He loves us because of who He is.

I could be the ugliest person in the world and He would still love me. I could be the poorest person in the world and He would still love me. I could have wasted my life on the streets, abused my body or even committed some crime and He would still love me. Job asked this question, "What is man that You magnify him, And that You are concerned about him?" (Job 7:17 NASB).

I would like to go back to verse six of this first chapter to the Philippians. I said that Paul was confident or convinced that God who had begun the good work would ultimately complete it. I think if I were to identify the central piece of this letter to the Philippians, the very thing that holds all of this in place, it would here in this sixth verse.

If we are not convinced that God is working in our lives, if we continually have doubts, then there is no possible way we can have confidence as we take this journey. There is no way we will have an attitude of joy in our lives. Everything we do in this Christian life must always have this understanding that it is God who has initiated the purpose and process and it is played out in our lives. I can't see how a

Christian can have such assurance if it does not begin with the truth that God is initiating the work.

Servitude means nothing if God is not the basis for serving. We do not have the right to decide when and to whom we will serve. It is totally against everything that God is. God shows His love to everyone and we need to do likewise. There can be no exceptions or distinctions. It is equally unrealistic to think that we can have confidence when we are refusing to work within God's will. We will always have this uncertainty about ourselves when we follow our own selfish ways, when we choose our own direction.

So when we come to verse six we need to have this understanding that joy comes when God is in control, when He is leading and guiding our lives. We know that God is working in our lives when we work within the sphere of His good work. Then and only then do we have joy.

This leads me into this idea of love. Paul writes, "So it is right that I should feel as I do about all of you, for you have a special place in my heart. You share with me the special favor of God, both in my imprisonment and in defending and confirming the truth of the Good News. God knows how much I love you and long for you with the tender compassion of Christ Jesus" (Phil. 1:7-8 NLT).

Realistically, love is something we fall short of in our understanding. As I said before, we use this word carelessly and fail to understand its power and potential. Love, like servitude and confidence, must always find its foundation on the good work that God has begun. In other words, we know that we are in God's will, we know that God is working in us when His good work is being manifested in our lives. So the indication that we are truly on this journey to joy comes from knowing that God is working within us.

So here are some indicators that God is working within us. Several things come to mind. First, we express the love of God in our lives because we have experienced it. Paul says that "It is right that I should feel as I do." Why is it right? Why is it right to feel totally different from the way we really want to feel? Because if God is truly working in us, the love we have for others comes from the love of God through us. Paul tells the Christians in Rome, " . . . for we know how dearly God loves us, and we feel this warm love everywhere within us because God has given us the Holy Spirit to fill our hearts with his love" (Rom. 5:5 TLB).

You see, it is God's love that pours out of us. You and I naturally are very selective when it comes to sharing our love and even then we only share a part of it. We decide where our love goes. This is the truth about human love, it is always selective and temporal. **Human love runs out, but God's love pours out**. Do you ever wonder why there are so many divorces out there? Why many seek for a relationship somewhere else? Why parents leave their children or abuse them? Human love can only go so far.

Here is a second truth, love sees the value in others. Jesus said, "My command is this: Love each other as I have loved you. Greater love has no one than this, that he lay down his life for his friends" (John 15:12-13 NIV). It's no wonder that Paul says these people had a **"special place"** in his heart. In the Greek it means that he was holding them in his heart in the same way the Philippian Christians were holding Paul in their hearts.

He says that they had this special place because they had ministered to him during his imprisonment and in defending the Gospel. But, they also had a special place because of their relationship with Christ. It has to be that way with Christians. We need to have a special place in our hearts for each other. Whether in good or bad times we need to help each other, pray for each other and share in the defense and propagation of the gospel.

A third thing to consider is that love finds its foundation in Jesus Christ. In times of greatest need we sometimes take our eyes off of God and put them on ourselves. But love looks beyond our simple lives and sees "with tender compassion of Christ" the needs of others. When Jesus was hanging on the cross, He didn't complain or criticize, He simply said this, "When Jesus saw his mother standing there beside the disciple he loved, he said to her, 'Dear woman, here is your son.' And he said to this disciple, 'Here is your mother.' And from then on this disciple took her into his home." (John 19:26-27 NLT).

There are times when it's really difficult to see the needs of those around us. We have a tendency to get all wrapped up in our own misery. We have a tendency to overlook the needs of a world that is in worse shape than we are. We all have this tendency to wallow in our own misery. We are human and sometimes that gets in the way of our spiritual discernment.

Paul writes in his second letter to the Corinthians about the Macedonians who, although they were facing difficult trials, willingly gave and even begged to give. They saw the needs of others more important than the things they were facing. "Though they have been going through much trouble and hard times, they have mixed their wonderful joy with their deep poverty, and the result has been an overflow of giving to others" (2 Cor. 8:2 TLB).

You see, the love of God goes beyond our expectations when we willingly allow God to move us with compassion for others. We know that God is working in our lives when His love overcomes our selfishness. We know God is working in our lives when we value others more than ourselves. Knowing this causes us to have confidence, leads us to have a heart for service and convinces us that He is leading and is in control.

Now the real test that God's love is working in our lives is the fact that we pray for the growth of other Christians. I can't think of anything that demonstrates selfishness more than this, that as Christians we refuse, not forget, but we refuse to pray for the spiritual growth of others. Paul goes on to say, "I pray that your love may over flow" and "that you keep growing in knowledge and understanding" (v.9). Wow! What a heart. Paul was going to die and here he prays for these Christians to continue to mature in their spiritual walk. He prays that love continues to overflow like an unending flood. Paul isn't looking for some small level of love but the perfection of that love.

Paul never asks anyone to do something that he wouldn't do or hasn't done. This letter is a heartfelt letter. He has lived this life. He has sacrificed, he has served, and he has loved. If every person who calls themselves a Christian would have a heart like Paul, think of where the church would be today. Think about how effective and vibrant and powerful God's ministry would be.

But look again with me, this love is not some mindless effort guided by foolish feelings. This love Paul wants to overflow in their lives comes by *growing in knowledge and understanding*. What does he mean here by growing in knowledge and understanding? Love finds its basis in the Word of God. Love is God as the Bible tells us. If that is true, real love comes from knowing the things of God. The Bible reveals the nature and character of God. We have to take His Word and study the things about God, who He is and what He does. We learn the things concerning God. That is why it is so important for teachers to be well-prepared when leading in Bible study. Nothing upsets me more than to sit under teachers who have spent little time or effort in preparing to teach the Word of God to others.

As believers we need to know why it is necessary to love and how love should be manifested. For us to say we love people without any real reason or knowledge as to why is just plain foolish. As we read the Word of God we see God showing and demonstrating His love for us. We see it in His guidance of the Israelites in the Old Testament. We see God's love in the life, death and resurrection of His Son. We see it in the life of the church. God is love and He spares no expense to shower us with this love. That love can only be known through His Word and in our personal experience with Him.

We experience God's love flowing out of us. We see God working in us and through us when we live our lives within the sphere of His love. The Apostle John writes, "If we love our Christian brothers and sisters, it proves that we have passed from death to life. But a person who has no love is still dead" (1 John 3:14 NLT). That really is the potential that love creates in us as we live it and share it with others. It proves to others and to the world that God is real and that God really loves us. So love is an important element in the Christian journey.

Paul says that we are not only to have knowledge, but also understanding. Here, this understanding can best be understood as having wisdom or discernment. Just having the knowledge is not enough. Having this knowledge and knowing how to apply it is what Paul is really getting at. I find it quite humorous when I read some political bloggers who think they know what Christians should believe and how they should act. They believe the Christian life should be lived a certain way. Yet they choose not to be Christians because they think Christians are hypocrites.

So what does Paul mean when he says we need this understanding? Well, the Greek word means to know the difference between what is true and what is not. What is good and what is not. What is essential and what is not essential. It distinguishes between what is important and what is not important. In the case of love, we must always be sure what true love is and what human love is. The writer of Hebrews says, "Solid food is for those who are mature, who through training have the skill to recognize the difference between right and wrong" (Heb. 5:14 NLT).

Do you know why Paul says this? Here's why. "For I want you to understand what really matters" (v.10a). What really matters? Church cleanliness? More people sitting in the pews? More money coming in? Names, titles, traditions? What really matters to you? Too many times the emphasis is placed on getting and not growing.

It's really heartbreaking to say that what really matters to most of us is our space, our time, our comfort and our traditions. Many Christians today have a hard time displaying a heart of warmth and purpose. Yet, we are called upon by Scripture to cultivate a heart much like Paul and it begins with giving our hearts to Christ. We cannot get a heart of love by joining a certain church, by observing certain traditions or fulfilling some church requirement.

Let me be very clear here, if you are placing your hope of eternal salvation on the membership of any church, it will only lead you to eternal hell. I have never read in the Word of God that you have to belong to a certain denomination. Nowhere in the Scriptures are you going to find that religion alone can lead you to heaven. Only membership in the family of God leads to eternal peace and that begins with a relationship with Jesus Christ.

Don't misunderstand me here. I am not saying that you shouldn't belong to a body of believers. I am not saying that every denomination is evil. What I am saying is that if you are a member of a church and you do not have a personal relationship with Christ your membership alone cannot get you into heaven. I am a member of Emmanuel Baptist Church here in Tucson. But that membership does not guarantee me eternal life. It simply means that I identify with that body of believers. Only Jesus can guarantee me eternal life.

So what really matters to Paul? Paul says this is what matters, "the righteous character produced in your life by Jesus Christ"(v.11b). All these other things are worthless if they do not produce the character of Jesus Christ in your life. We can serve till our heart wears out, but if it doesn't produce godly character, it's worthless. We can have all the confidence in the world and love until we can't love anymore and all that still wouldn't produce godly character. Isaiah writes, " . . . all our righteous acts are like filthy rags . . . " (Isa. 64:6 NIV).

How do we get this "righteous character?" By living "pure and blameless lives until the day of Christ's return" (v.10b). What does that mean? Now these two words "pure and blameless" describe the type of lives we should be living in the sphere of God's good work in us. First the word "pure" carries the idea of being "judged by sunlight." You and I know that when we try to see something in the dark, we can't tell if it's good or bad. If we're looking to buy a used car, it's probably a good thing to look at it in the daylight, right? That way we can see all the dings and dents on it.

When I worked for Reproductions Inc., the building we were in was fairly old. It was red brick, but the bricks had been worn away by the weather. The company decided to put up a new facade so that the store would not look so old and beat up, but rather have a good representation. But the fact was, while it look good on the outside, the backside was still old and worn out. That is the idea here that there can be no masks or facade about us. We need to live in the light of Christ's character. This is how a lot of us like to live, with a facade over us while inside we are really filled with sin. But so what? Who can see through this facade? God does and really He is the One we should be concerned about. We may fool a lot of people and I should know. I have played that game, but God always knows and He always sees. David says, "Who may ascend into the hill of the Lord? And who may stand in His holy place? He who has clean hands and a pure heart, Who has not lifted up his soul to falsehood And has not sworn deceitfully" (Ps. 24:3-4 NASB).

"How can a young man keep his way pure? By keeping it according to Your word" (Ps. 119:9 NASB).

"Blessed are the pure in heart, for they shall see God" (Matt. 5:8 NASB).

Now the second word "blameless" carries the idea of "not causing to stumble." That's pretty simple. If we are living according to God's will and purpose we will keep ourselves from making dumb choices and not stumbling. When we are living the Christ-like life we will also not be a stumbling block to someone else. Paul said, "We live in such a way that no one will stumble because of us, and no one will find fault with our ministry" (2 Cor. 6:3 NLT).

This is a daily practice, not a Sunday only thing. Paul goes on to say, "until the day of Christ's return." This is not always easy. Many times we've been tempted to cut corners or take a shortcut just because it's a struggle to maintain our spiritual walk. Paul encouraged the Galatian Christians, "So let's not get tired of doing what is good. At just the right time we will reap a harvest of blessing if we don't give up" (Gal. 6:9 NLT).

Then finally Paul says this, "May you always be filled with the fruit of your salvation—the righteous character produced in your life by Jesus Christ—for this will bring much glory and praise to God" (v.11 NASB). "Being filled with the fruit of your salvation" could mean that we are satisfied with who we are and the life we are living. This satisfaction comes by knowing that we are growing into Christ-likeness. Here then is the ultimate goal of living the Christian life, "for this will bring much glory and praise to God." That is the ultimate goal of living the Christian life—pleasing God.

Here's the reward, first there will be a fullness of joy knowing that God is working in our lives. Second, we will become more like Christ the more we yield our lives to Him. This ultimately leads me to mature with a heart of gratitude. This is what we will look at in the coming chapter. Paul says that what brings glory and praise to God is a heart that feels, a heart that loves, a heart that desires, a heart that prays and a heart that seeks. Do you have that kind of heart today?

# 4

# The Journey Of Gratitude
# Philippians 1:12-20

It's amazing to me that even though Paul was in prison he had this unshakeable attitude of gratitude. If it had been me I would have been looking for the best lawyer to get me out of there. I can't imagine what it would be like to be in prison for any length of time. Well, if the truth be known I've been to Florence State Prison here in Arizona, **not** as a resident, **but** as a guest. I did two live concerts there. It was the most frightening experience of my life. When those big gates closed behind me and we were escorted to the hall by enormous guys carrying huge rifles, I was scared out of my mind.

Nothing had prepared me for what prison life was like or for the current residents that lived there. I am sure that those who resided there were there for a good reason. While we were there we met a man who had committed murder. He was a nice guy, but I really didn't want to get too close to him. Then there was another guy who had murdered his family. Wow! I bet he was fun at family gatherings.

These men had made bad choices in life. I'm sure, that by the standard of the law, they deserved to be there. Some, I must say, had given their hearts to Christ while in prison. Even though they knew they were not going to be released, they had already been set free from their sinful choices. Most of us really can't see the prison we create when we sin against the Father. Even though we are free on the outside, inside we are bound by the wrong choices we have made.

Paul had made wrong choices early in his life, but on the road to Damascus he made the right choice. He was going the wrong way and God had to get him to see his error and change his course. I don't think he ever forgot or ever stopped thanking the Lord for what took place in his life that night. Can you imagine if God had not convicted Paul's heart, where he would be today? I shudder to think of what life would be like without Jesus.

Paul's only reason for being in prison was his faithfulness to God. He was living in the sphere of God's will and for that he was imprisoned. Listen, you and I will encounter hardship when we truly live in the sphere of God's will. The Christian life is not all a walk in a rose garden. We cannot be a Christian and assume that the world is going to like us. If it didn't like Jesus, it certainly isn't going to like us.

Earlier this year some very radical people from the gay community invaded, mocked and tried to destroy several churches across America. There are other organizations as well striving to rip apart the religious community. So if you think that being a Christian in this day and age is easy, you have the wrong idea about Christianity or you have a very confused idea of the Word of God.

Jesus prayed, "But now I come to You; and these things I speak in the world so that they may have My joy made full in themselves. I have given them Your word; and the world has hated them, because they are not of the world, even as I am not of the world. I do not ask You to take them out of the world, but to keep them from the evil one" (John 17:13-15 NASB). Jesus had no illusion about how the world would treat believers and neither should we.

So while Paul was in prison about to lose his head, he had an amazing perspective. He was in this bad situation but he saw the overwhelming results of good taking place. He said, "Now I want you to know, brethren, that my circumstances have turned out for the greater progress of the gospel" (Phil 1:12 NASB). That is Christian character at its highest. He didn't whine or complain, he rejoiced. Do we rejoice when faced with unwelcome situations? Or do we whine and complain to God? How should we respond?

We should always respond with a heart of gratitude. But why? First, Paul said that a positive response to life situations can cause the Gospel to flourish. Listen to what he said, "So that my imprisonment in the cause of Christ has become well known throughout the whole praetorian guard and to everyone else" (Philip. 1:13 NASB). People are influenced in this world by either the positive or negative response we give when faced with unwelcome or unexpected life situations.

Now just imagine with me, Paul with two guys chained on either side of him. Who do you think was more influential? Wrong, not the guards, but Paul. I can just hear him as he prays and these guys have nowhere to go. "Dear God, I know that these two men are just doing their jobs but I pray that you will have mercy on their souls and that you will convict them of their evil ways. Amen!"

They hear this prayer over and over again. Then they go home and start telling their wives about what is happening at the office, but more specifically about Paul and his prayers, his conversations, and his writings. You still don't think he made a difference? He does and he tells us he does. "So that my imprisonment in the cause of Christ has become well known throughout the whole praetorian guard and to everyone else."

We know that God is working in our lives when we have the attitude of gratitude. We could be standing in the midst of the most severe crisis and yet have a thankful heart. We obviously aren't thankful for the trial or the crisis. If we're normal we would prefer that God test us in other ways. But more importantly we are grateful; we have this attitude of gratitude that He has counted us worthy to suffer for His name's sake.

Paul tells the Thessalonian Christians, "All this is evidence that God's judgment is right, and as a result you will be counted worthy of the kingdom of God, for which you are suffering" (2 Thess. 1:5 NIV). Peter tells the believers he is writing to, "However, if you suffer as a Christian, do not be ashamed, but praise God that you bear that name" (1 Pet. 4:16 NIV).

Second, he says that a positive response to our life situations can encourage others in their times of difficulties. Again, Paul says in verse 14; "And that most of the brethren, trusting in the Lord because of my imprisonment, have far more courage to speak the word of God without fear."

Not everything that happens in life to God's children, and more specifically to us, is always good. Some things are very hurtful, heartbreaking and difficult to handle. The death of a loved one, a tragedy, a divorce, abuse or financial collapse—when these things come unexpectedly, they are not easily dismissed. How we choose to handle them reveals our true dependence on the grace of God. Paul knew this and he placed his trust and life in the hands of the One who could deliver him. God had reassured him, "My grace is sufficient for you, for power is perfected in weakness" (2 Cor. 12:9 NASB).

We grow in our unwavering trust in God when we know that He is doing a good work in our lives. This is not only helpful in personal hardship but also needful in personal attacks. Again, listen to what Paul says, "Some, to be sure, are preaching Christ even from envy and strife, but some also from good will; the latter do it out of love, knowing that I am appointed for the defense of the gospel; the former proclaim Christ out of selfish ambition rather than from pure motives, thinking to cause me distress in my imprisonment" (vs.15-17 NASB).

Isn't it just like us, when someone is down we kick them a few more times? These self-righteous proclaimers were trying to embarrass Paul because he was in prison and they weren't. Sometimes we hurt people further by trying to explain why they may be facing difficult situations. We reason that maybe they were not following God, or that if they had been following God more closely, they might not be in that situation. Whatever the reason, Paul says, "So what?" No matter why they did it, how they did it, or where they did it, he saw Christ being preached. "What then? Only that in every way, whether in pretense or in truth, Christ is proclaimed; and in this I rejoice. Yes, and I will rejoice" (v.18 NASB).

No matter what happens in life we should always have an attitude of gratitude. Why? Why should we as Christians be grateful for our life experiences? Because it's God's way of showing Himself to this sinful world. When we allow Him to shape us even in the hardships of life, we show those around us that He cares and has all the resources to meet all our needs. When we trust in Him, even in the most difficult moments, He changes us according to His image. We don't see the complete picture or His ultimate purpose, but one day we will. Paul said; "But we all, with unveiled face, beholding as in a mirror the glory of the Lord, are being transformed into the same image from glory to glory, just as from the Lord, the Spirit" (2 Cor. 3:18 NASB95).

This is why I believe verse six of this first chapter is so important. Without the full confidence that God is working in our lives, that God is doing a good work in us, we can't have any real peace or real assurance about our circumstances. Paul says, " . . . for I know that this will turn out for my deliverance through your prayers and the provision of the Spirit of Jesus Christ, according to my earnest expectation and hope, that I will not be put to shame in anything, but that with all boldness,

Christ will even now, as always, be exalted in my body, whether by life or by death" (vs.19-20 NASB).

He says "He knows." Now that is something every Christian should know about the spiritual life. By experience we should know that God is working in our lives. We should know that other believers are interceding on our behalf. We should know and sense that the Holy Spirit is working in the circumstances of our lives.

When we know that, we have confidence as Paul did, that we will be delivered. It may not be in this life, but in the life to come, but we will be delivered. Also notice that Paul states that he has expectations of that happening. He says, "for I know that this will turn out for my deliverance." He has his hope firmly fixed on the promise that, "Whosoever believes on the Lord Jesus Christ will be saved."

Finally he says he will not be disappointed. In the Greek the word "shame or ashamed" is best translated "disappointed." While there were those that sought to shame Paul or ridicule him and his beliefs, he says "I know by experience that everything I have done I have done believing that God is and that God rewards." We can't make this journey with a partial belief. Either we know or we don't know. We either have experienced Christ or we have not experienced Him. The evidence is in our lives. How we respond to life's circumstances, whether they are good or difficult, will reveal whether God is truly working in and through our lives.

But I think the ultimate evidence of a grateful heart is who gets the glory. Paul says again, "That with all boldness, Christ will even now, as always, be exalted in my body, whether by life or by death" (v.20 NASB). You see our lives are to be lived for the sake of testifying for the Lord Jesus Christ. What we do and how we do it reveals what we believe about Jesus and His Word. If we are called upon to suffer for Christ's sake then we should be willing to rejoice. Not because we are immune to the pain or callous to the situation, but because it is only for a season.

Paul tells the Christians in Rome, "And since we are his children, we will share his treasures—for all God gives to his Son Jesus is now ours too. But if we are to share his glory, we must also share his suffering. Yet what we suffer now is nothing compared to the glory he will give us later" (Rom. 8:17-18 TLB).

Peter says, "But even if you should suffer for the sake of righteousness, you are blessed. And do not fear their intimidation, and do not be troubled" (1 Pet. 3:14 NASB).

John writes, "Do not fear what you are about to suffer. Behold, the devil is about to cast some of you into prison, so that you will be tested, and you will have tribulation for ten days. Be faithful until death, and I will give you the crown of life" (Rev. 2:10 NASB).

I understand that it's very hard to have an attitude of gratitude when things are not going our way. It seems that living right only leads to more discomfort or uncertainty. Don't lose heart. In this journey to joy if you'll just look ahead you'll see this, "And He will wipe away every tear from their eyes; and there will no longer be any death; there will no longer be any mourning, or crying, or pain; the first things have passed away" (Rev. 21:4 NASB).

# 5

# The Journey Of Decision
# Philippians 1:21-26

Have you ever been pulled in two different directions? You want to go this way but something in your heart just keeps pulling in the other direction? There are times in this life we have the stress of not knowing which is better. Every day we are prodded to make decisions. We have to decide when to get up. We have to decide whether or not to brush our teeth. We have to decide if we are going to work. We make each of these decisions with little or no thought behind them. We do this daily.

But there are other decisions we have to make that have long-term implications. We have to decide to obey the laws so that we do not intentionally harm anyone or ourselves. We have to decide whether we as Christians are going to live godly or foolishly in our daily walk. This decision isn't always that easy.

I remember sometime back, my brother and I went to Western Auto (those of you who are old enough, remember what this was). Western Auto was a sort of general store. It carried tools, hardware, sporting goods, sort of like Sears. The store was within walking distance of our house.

My brother and I were going to this store for only one reason—we wanted to buy fishing lures. Now, you need to know that we have never lived by any water, unless you count the arroyos that flourish around the city during the monsoon season. On top of that, we had never been fishing. The closest I ever came to a fish was at the supermarket where they were displayed at the meat counter.

But it didn't matter. We had decided that was what we were going to buy and that was what we did. I need to make a confession here. We only had a few dollars between us and we didn't want to blow it all on fishing lures. So we had a plan or you could say "we made a decision." The plan was to buy a few lures and pocket a few. That seemed like a good plan.

So we initiated the plan and stuck what we could in our pockets. If you know what a lure is you know that it has three to four sharp points on it. I can't really describe the pain I experienced when these lures attached themselves to my inner thighs. It seemed like it took forever getting to the counter to pay. I had tears in my eyes so I tried really hard to paste a smile on my face.

At the counter the sales clerk took what I was paying for and asked me if I wanted him to put the lures in a bag or if I just wanted to put them in my pocket. I smiled and said "Bag please!" Sort of like Don Corleone. When we were done we walked as quickly as we could out the door and into an alleyway. We then proceeded to pry these things off our thighs. I've often wondered if the clerk really knew what we had done.

Sometimes our decisions bring about pain. Yet we have the potential to avoid this pain. Just like the clerk at the store who probably knew what we had done, God also sees and knows what we do and have done. He sees the choices we make and He knows the pain that comes from some of those choices.

Paul also had this tug of war within himself. He longed for the freedom to be released from this world and more specifically from the pain that he was going through. Yet, he contemplated the benefits of leaving or staying. He says, "For to me, to live is Christ" (Phil. 1:21).

That's an amazing statement. He said life is nothing without Jesus. Living isn't living if Christ doesn't reside within you. But that isn't the way most of us live, is it? We live for Christ when it's convenient and we whine when it gets difficult. Paul was facing death. He knew that he didn't have much longer, but even if he didn't, the life he had at that moment was for Christ. Let me ask you, are you living for Jesus at this very moment?

The truth is that as long as life is going okay, sometimes Christ is not all that high on the priority list. But if you were told today that you only had so many months to live, I would venture a guess that as a Christian you would go out and do all you could for Jesus. Let's look at this statement for a minute. Paul says, "For to me to live is Christ and to die is gain." First he says, "for me to live." This is really an amazing statement. It is this confession that truly reveals the person Paul is. Every decision that he makes is based on this statement.

What does he mean by this? Well, he first says life is really important. He sees that life is not something that happens at some point in time. Some of us are only living when things are going our way. When things don't pan out in our lives, we basically stop living. But Paul says life is lived moment by moment. So what is life? *It is the very essence of daily Christian living in the sphere of God's will.* Looking back at Paul's life we see that from the moment of that Damascus encounter he never stopped short of this life. He has lived it, suffered for it and is now facing death because of it.

I find it very distressing when I see Christians who have given up on this life. They see themselves without any hope. They think that God is done with them because their lives are not what they should be. But the fact is, that many times when Christians give up on the journey, it's because they have charted their own course. They have made ministry conform to their wishes. So when it doesn't work out for them, they fall by the wayside.

I am also fearful of some evangelistic programs that give unbelievers a false sense of security. I am fearful of some denominations that make membership a prerequisite for getting into the kingdom. I am fearful when religious philosophies and traditions take the place of the Gospel message we have been given to preach. "For me to live." This is what we need to consider, Paul says.

We need to stop preaching and teaching that the Christian life is something that will make us better people. It doesn't. We are not a better person the moment we accept Jesus. Giving our hearts to Christ is not like taking some medication to make us feel better. That's the problem I see coming out of some pulpits and Bible Studies. They teach that all we need to do is get Jesus in our hearts and we're good to go. The truth is the Christian life is a progressive growth into Christ-likeness. It is a daily process and anything short of this is a misconception of Holy Scripture.

Here is a second thing, Paul says, "For me to live is Christ." Nothing is more important in life than for the Christian to be living for Christ. Paul doesn't live for Paul. Paul doesn't even live for the Church or his ministry. He lives for Christ. How often do we live our lives with that in mind? The road to joy must always have Christ as the ultimate goal. Paul writes to Timothy, "For it is for this we labor and strive, because we have fixed our hope on the living God, who is the Savior of all men, especially of believer" (1 Tim. 4:10 NASB).

The word "strive" in the Greek is "agônizomai" and it means "to fight." In the New Testament it had the imagery of a contest. It is often used in connection with the athlete. The athlete fights through the urges to give up, take shortcuts or somehow compromise in order to succeed in obtaining the ultimate prize. We can't have the mindset of Paul, "For me to live is Christ," unless we are willing to discipline ourselves for this journey. If we don't, then as soon as we get started on this journey, we will either try and look for the shortcuts, or just flat out give up.

That is why we need to devote ourselves to giving the sense of the Word and not just the milk of the Word. At some point in time milk is just not enough, we need meat. Jesus never gave the idea that the road to the Christian life was easy. He said, "Strive to enter through the narrow door; for many, I tell you, will seek to enter and will not be able" (Luke 13:24 NASB).

Then Paul says, "For me to live is Christ and to die is gain." What can possibly be gained by dying? For nonbelievers there is not much to gain in death. But for the believer there is always abundance. Paul says that his gain would be eternal fellowship with Christ. Heaven is a grand place. When we stop and think about it there is no more sorrow, no more tears, no more aches and pain. Life in the eternal is a place where life is lived to the fullest.

So Paul looks beyond his circumstances and sees the benefits of being in heaven. But Paul never lets the splendor of heaven diminish his hope for greater success in propagating the Gospel in the world in which he is still living. He says, "Yet to remain on in the flesh is more necessary for your sake." Then he says again in verses 25 & 26, "Convinced of this, I know that I will remain and continue with you all for your progress and joy in the faith, so that your proud confidence in me may abound in Christ Jesus through my coming to you again."

He sees that if he were given the opportunity to continue in this life it would yield fruitful labor and it would benefit the believers. He sees God's blessing through new opportunities if God lets him live. "This will mean fruitful labor for me." He sees conversions taking place. He sees new churches started somewhere else. He sees opportunities in the midst of a crisis.

That is a heart on a joy journey. He has joy, not because of his circumstances, but because of his relationship to the Lord. That is a good problem to struggle with—to be in heaven with Christ or to take advantage of the opportunities here through Christ. That was probably the hardest decision he had faced up to this point. "But I am hard-pressed from both directions, having the desire to depart and be with Christ, for that is very much better; yet to remain on in the flesh is more necessary for your sake" (vs. 21-24 NASB95).

Are you where Christ wants you to be? Do you have a heart like Paul that you could say, "For to me, to live is Christ and to die is gain?"

> "I will give them hearts that recognize me as the Lord.
> They will be my people, and I will be their God,
> for they will return to me wholeheartedly."
> (Jeremiah 24:7 NLT)

# 6

# Conclusion
# Philippians 1:27-30

"Whatever!" Have you ever heard this phrase? You may say something to your wife in an argument and she may respond, "Whatever!" Or you may be in a disagreement with your neighbor and you turn away and mutter under your breath, "Whatever!" We do it simply because we don't want to continue any disagreement. We do it simply because we aren't getting our way.

In his closing remarks of this first chapter, Paul says "Whatever!" Only he's not in any disagreement with anyone. Paul is simply saying, "Considering all I have written up to this point, whatever happens, whether I am there or not, live your life in this manner." I guess you might look at this as Paul simply saying, "Stay focused."

In this journey focus is very important. We can lose our focus and wind up in a ditch somewhere. I once read where a young man driving a trolley lost his focus and wound up in an accident. It only takes a second when driving, to get into an accident simply by taking our eyes off the road or, in this case, the journey.

We began this section by mentioning some of the hall of famers who took their eyes off the journey for a moment and wound up in trouble. David, Abraham, Moses and others who were on this journey, but for a second lost their focus. Just be glad God did not let you live in their time. Their mistakes, their car-in-the-ditch moments, have been recorded for all time. We have the benefit of learning from their experiences simply by reading their life stories.

But we also have those today who have been very prominent in the religious community who took their eyes off the journey. They've not only found themselves in a ditch, but have brought down others with them. We all have the potential of running into a ditch if we don't keep a watchful eye as we make this journey. John writes, "Watch out that you do not lose what you have worked for, but that you may be rewarded fully" (2 John 1:8 NIV).

With this in mind Paul writes, "Whatever happens, conduct yourselves in a manner worthy of the gospel of Christ" (v.27a NIV). Paul never bases his life on his feelings or wishes. He knows there's a possibility that God will let him live a few more years. But he also knows that he could be there in jail for a longer period of time or even face death. So, no matter what may happen, the Philippian believers were to continue to live in a certain way or conduct.

On this journey to joy we are going to be faced with many uncertainties. This is life and life just happens. Christians are not singled out to suffer while unbelievers go through life untouched. Life happens no matter what your spiritual position is. Jesus said, "He causes His sun to rise on the evil and the good, and sends rain on the righteous and the unrighteous" (Matt. 5:45 NASB). In other words, believers experience heartaches and hardships just like unbelievers do.

So Paul reiterates what he has been saying in this first chapter. We must have this certain conduct in our lives, "Conduct yourselves in a manner worthy of the Gospel of Christ" (v.27). In the original language the thought is "to live as a citizen as in respect to your birth place or country." Here it means to live as a member of the family of God.

That isn't always easy, is it? While living in the here and now there are so many things that pull us in one direction or another. So we come to a **decision**, to either live as a member of society or to live as a member of God's family? To live for ourselves or for God? It's a choice, a decision, which we need to make daily. Jesus said, "If any of you wants to be my follower, you must turn from your selfish ways, take up your cross daily, and follow me" (Luke 9:23 NLT).

My decisions on this journey to joy have not always been the smartest or the most honorable. At times it has been costly. As I look back at the times I wound up in a ditch or a dead end it was because I was using my self-created GPS (getting pridefully stupid). Joshua said to his people, "Choose today whom you will serve" (Joshua 24:15 NLT).

So in this journey, this life, we have to consciously make a decision every day as to how we will live our lives, how or whom we will represent in our daily walk. This choice reflects who we are really trying to please. Paul shows us the right direction for our choices, which is to trust in Jesus for everyday joyful living.

He says again, "Conduct yourselves in a manner worthy of the Gospel of Christ." How should we base our daily decisions? By truly being a representative of the Gospel, the essence of the character of God and Jesus Christ. What is the Gospel? Well, it is basically Good News.

In our world today we really need some good news. There are so many things that are ripping us apart. The Christian community holds the secret to living life in times of great uncertainty. Christians have to be seen as representatives of a life-changing message. The only Jesus this world will ever see is through Christian behavior. So we have to decide daily whom we are going to represent, ourselves or Jesus?

This leads us to consider the next behavior of conduct, which is **gratitude**. Paul says, "For it has been granted to you on behalf of Christ not only to believe on him, but also to suffer for him" (v.29 NIV). Some people would look at this and say, "Why should I be grateful in my sufferings?" When we only look at our present condition, when we only see what we are going through and how that affects us, then we don't cultivate an attitude of gratitude. We just proceed to have a pity party.

But here is another way to look at it. I admit that sometimes it's been hard for me to look at any suffering as a joy or a pleasure. As I read these verses I realized that God found me worthy to suffer for His sake. To put a different way, God entrusted me with this moment of suffering, not because He was trying to get even or break me, but because of what it would yield. In a sense, it's a privilege to be counted suitable for the task.

Just because life isn't going the way I want it to go, or just because I am in a time of uncertainty or suffering doesn't mean God is angry or getting His revenge on me because of the life choices I have made. To me, it means He has entrusted something very special to me. He has confidence in me that I will be able to produce the fruit He is looking for. When I think about it in those terms, then I am really grateful. I have this attitude of gratitude because He has counted me worthy of suffering for His sake. James says, "Consider it pure joy, my brothers, whenever you face trials of many kinds" (James 1:2 NIV).

Paul was not alone in his sufferings and neither are we. He says, "Since you are going through the same struggle you saw I had, and now hear that I still have" (v.30 NIV). We, like Paul, have this connection with other believers. At times we will experience suffering, but when we do, there are those who are praying for us. That is what Paul experienced with the Philippian Christians. We really have each other and God really cares about our life situations.

I am convinced this is why Paul says, "I will know that you stand firm in one spirit" (v.27c NIV). Here is the essence of Christian unity, *love*. We cannot have any firm footing in the Christian community if we are constantly fighting with one another. Neither will we have any assurance that we are standing firm in anything we do, including the Gospel.

While serving as an Associate Pastor and a Senior Pastor, I have seen people leave the church and the church split over silly things. Listen, most of the disagreements in the church are really foolish. Someone leaves because of the music or the method or the message. Some hold grudges over foolish things like philosophies or practices or denominational traditions.

However, we are called upon to love. We are expected to live like Jesus. We are to be the Living Gospel to a lost and dying world. Because of our pettiness, though, we are seen as foolish and useless, lacking the Christian conduct the world expects to see. Why would anyone give their heart to Jesus if their life is no different from the lives they see Christians living? Are your toes hurting, too?

Jesus called us to love one another and Paul calls us to stand firm together in one spirit. What is more important to you, having it your way? If that's how you feel and that's how you live your Christian life, then maybe you need to join the Burger King Ministry. Its philosophy is "You can have it your way!"

There are plenty of churches out there that cater to the Burger King mentality. If we want to have success and want to avoid the ditch along the way, though, we have to have love and the desire to stand firm with other believers. That, my friends, takes a willingness to work with one another, listen to one another, serve one another and learn with one another.

In the Gospel message there is no room for pettiness or selfishness. The success of any ministry is not based on the preacher, the buildings, the people or the money, but love. Time does not permit me to talk about 1 Corinthians 13, the love chapter. Let me say this, you can be the smoothest talker, the sharpest dresser, the most glorious voice in the choir or the most generous giver, but without love none of these things matter. Paul says, "The greatest of these is love" (I Cor. 13:13 NIV). Jesus also said, "Love each other. Just as I have loved you . . . Your love for one another will prove to the world that you are my disciples" (John 13:34-35 NLT).

Now that leads us to this—*servitude*—"Contending as one man for the faith of the gospel" (v.27d NIV). Servitude is basically the outcome of love. When we love one another, we willingly serve one another. To "contend" means basically to "strive to, or to strive together."

We have been given a mandate to proclaim the Gospel. By proclaiming it we not only preach it, teach it, speak and write about it, **we live it**. One of the greatest temptations we have, especially in leadership, is to think that we must be served. Look at our political system and you will find that some politicians feel that the American people are there to serve them. We see it in businesses and in families, as well. The fact of the matter is that as Christians we are called to serve, not be served. When we exhibit the essence of servitude to one another then are we contending for the faith together.

Finally, when our conduct exemplifies these qualities—service, gratitude, love and right decision-making—what follows next is the certainty of "*confidence*." Paul says again, "Without being frightened in any way by those who oppose you" (v.28a NIV). There will be those that oppose the Christian community. If you ever venture to any of the political blogs very seldom are you going to find anyone standing up for the Christian conservative. As a matter of fact, they see Christians as hypocrites, bigots and racists. They are distrustful of anything to do with Jesus or God. I am deeply concerned about the state of the church today. It seems that the church has not made much of a difference in this country in the last twenty years.

I'm also amazed at the spiritual condition of our country. Why is that? I think partly because our Government has been very active in making everything and everyone equal. It seems everything has to be Politically Correct. If you are not P.C. then you must be a racist or a bigot. Our world is changing and not for the better. Things we considered shameful or sinful are now being played out in full view of everyone. Humanist organizations have been emboldened to speak out against anything to do with Christianity.

I also think this is taking place because the church in many ways has been shamed by its own scandals. The church is trying to be more in line with worldly lifestyles. We are trying to reach younger generations using the marketing savvy of today's businesses. We have taken the power and conviction of the Word, and made it more hearer-friendly.

Haven't we been called to speak the Word in truth and in love? There is such a thing as going too far for the sake of some religious mandate and we need to be careful about that. Yet, we are to preach the Word whether it's convenient or offensive. Paul said to "Preach the word in season or out of season, whether it is fashionable or not, preach the Word" (2 Tim.4:2). To the Corinthians Paul said this, "But if our gospel be hid, it is hid to them that are lost." (2 Cor. 4:3 KJV).

Preaching the Gospel, sharing the Good News with this world is still our priority. We cannot shy away from this and we should not fear any backlash from anyone or any group. We should not be fearful in doing the will of God. Peter said, "However, if you suffer as a Christian, do not be ashamed, but praise God that you bear that name . . . If you are insulted because of the name of Christ, you are blessed, for the Spirit of glory and of God rests on you" (1 Pet. 4:14 &16 NIV).

As the time for the return of Christ draws near, the war on Christians will intensify. Jesus said once again, "I've told you these things to prepare you for rough times ahead. They are going to throw you out of the meeting places. There will even come a time when anyone who kills you will think he's doing God a favor. They will do these things because they never really understood the Father. I've told you these things so that when the time comes and they start in on you, you'll be well-warned and ready for them" (John 16:1-4 MSG).

Peter even reminds his readers in his letter, "Dear friends, do not be surprised at the painful trial you are suffering, as though something strange were happening to you" (1 Pet. 4:12 NIV). It's going to happen, if it hasn't already. However, we should not be fearful or silent. If we truly believe that *GOD HAS BEGUN A GOOD WORK* in us, then we have nothing to fear. God will see us through all of this and that should give us immeasurable confidence. Peter goes on to say, "So then, those who suffer according to God's will should commit themselves to their faithful Creator and continue to do good" (1 Pet. 4:19 NIV).

We have a wonderful journey before us. At times it will seem like we've been on this journey forever, but when we take a look at God's roadmap, His Word, He tells us how it will all end. HE WINS! WE'RE HOME!

> "Well, we've nothing now to fear
> 'Cause we know Lord that You're here
> And this song we'll sing through all eternity
> We shall overcome
> By the blood of the Lamb
> Well, we shall overcome
> By the blood of the Lamb."
> ®&©David Ray/Still Water Publishing, 1995

# The Journey of Character

## Philippians 2

# 7

# The Journey Through Selflessness
# Philippians 2:1-4

In the summer of 1990 my wife and I and our three girls packed up the car and headed to Fort Worth, Texas. Early that year we felt God calling us to seminary. Before we left town that afternoon, we stopped by my parents' house to say goodbye. My dad hugged me and said goodbye with a look of uncertainty and yet understanding. I never thought it would be the last time I would see him. In December of that year he passed away.

It took a few years for me to get over the hurt and anger I felt, but as I look back through the corridors of time, I remember my dad as a hero and a model for me. My dad was a simple man. He really didn't need a lot and never asked for much. He worked hard all of his life. He was never boastful about things nor did he ever, as far as I can remember, cause an argument or seek revenge on anyone. He was generous, funny at times, and considerate of others. When there was a disagreement he did what he could to keep the peace.

He was not perfect by any means, but he was gentle, thoughtful and cautious. He raised 11 children and he dealt fairly with each of us. When we needed his help, he was there. When we were in financial difficulties, he gave. He never had a lot of money, but he always gave what he could. If there was one word I would use to describe him, well, it would be "selfless."

I can't say that I have lived my life like he did. There were times I was selfish, boastful, and arrogant. I can think of many times I was the cause of arguments. Someone once said I looked like my father. Not hardly! I can truly say I still have a lot to learn from him.

Do we really look like our Heavenly Father? I think that is the question I ask myself more and more the older I get. As children, we all tend to look like one parent more than the other. Sometimes it's the way we think, talk, act, or live our lives. As Christians this should be true of all of us if we truly believe God is our Father.

In this section of Philippians Paul is asking this same question, "Do you look like God the Father?" He says to the Philippian Christians, "If you have any encouragement from being united with Christ, if any comfort from his love, if any fellowship with the Spirit, if any tenderness and compassion, then make my joy complete by being like-minded, having the same love, being one in spirit and purpose. Do nothing out of selfish ambition or vain conceit, but in humility consider others better than yourselves. Each of you should look not only to your own interests, but also to the interests of others" (Phil. 2:1-4 NIV).

Paul has just finished telling the Philippian Christians that he is confident that nothing external, even his current circumstances, can rob him of his joy or the certainty of his relationship to the Lord. He has completely turned his life over to the fact that, if God through His power and purpose has begun this good work in his life, then God through His power and purpose will complete it. Simply put, his faith cannot be shaken. It is firmly grounded in the promise of Jesus Christ, "That whosoever believes in Him shall not perish but have everlasting life" (John 3:16 NKLV).

He begins here with this in mind. If the Christians at Philippi were truly concerned about his present condition, then they would not seek to add to that hardship by being at odds with each other. Paul says, rather in a nice way, "If you have any encouragement from being united with Christ . . . then make my joy complete" (vs. 1-2 NIV). Why would he have to say this to the very people who had been very supportive of him and his ministry?

I have been blessed to grow up in a tightly-knit family. This family has seen its share of personal tragedy and disagreements. While we may be close, with eleven children in the family, there is a matter of personalities and opinions. Each of us has various likes and dislikes, ranging from the political to the religious and such. There have been times we have been divided on certain situations where feelings have been hurt or words have been spoken that have caused divisions. However, we're still a family and, I suppose, we're normal.

It's the same in our world today. We live in a time of great uncertainty and many divisions. There is tension between various political parties which has impacted the feelings of the people around them and those who support them. Around the world, world leaders have their suspicions about each other and they are distrustful about anything or anyone.

Even the church today is not immune from such things. The churches around the world have these same battles, these same disagreements and divisions. While that should not be, it is, and it is very evident by the numerous church factions around us. The church is the one place where this should not be true, but it is and it has become a stumbling block to many.

The church at Philippi was no different. It is evident that while they cared for and loved Paul, there were still things in the church that needed to be addressed. It's foolish to think that just because we are Christians we don't have such problems. So what was the problem? Here is what Paul says, "Do nothing out of selfish ambition or vain conceit" (v.3a NIV).

This was the cause of disunity—*selfishness*. Selfishness is the cause of disunity in the world, in the church, and in our personal lives. It is the reason many churches split or breakup. It is the reason many marriages fail. It is the reason many countries do not get along and always want to war about things. Selfishness will destroy anything and everything that stands it its way. It's like a cancer.

Years ago I remember watching the movie "The Never Ending Story." It was about a boy whose lack of dreams had caused the *"Nothing"* to destroy a place called Fantasia. When the *"Nothing"* swept the land it left nothing but destruction behind it. Selfishness, like the Nothing, leaves destruction in its path. Paul tells the Corinthian church, "But, dear brothers, I beg you in the name of the Lord Jesus Christ to stop arguing among yourselves. Let there be real harmony so that there won't be splits in the church. I plead with you to be of one mind, united in thought and purpose" (1 Cor.1:10 TLB).

Listen, when we gave our hearts to Jesus, we were not automatically immune to selfishness. In fact, when we were saved, we were still the same people, had the same habits, and exhibited the same responses and sometimes acted foolishly. To put it simply, we were still sinners.

The only difference between us and a nonbeliever is that we were saved by grace. We were forgiven of our sinful past. We were washed by the blood of Jesus Christ, but we still had the propensity to sin.

This is where I have often gotten off course. I thought that as long as I had Jesus I would not be prone to such a life again. Maybe you have, too. That's why I think we often get off course on this journey to joy. We forget that we still live in a sinful world and we still have the potential to sin. Selfishness is the one character flaw we all have and many times refuse to let go. I know it is true in my life and it could very well be true in yours.

Paul addresses the core problem facing the Philippians, *selfish ambition* and *vain conceit*. Years ago when I worked for Reproductions, Inc., I had worked up to the position of salesperson for them. But it was not enough. So when another company wanted to open their business in town and give Reproductions a run for their money, well, I signed on. They promised me more money and a better position. I did everything I could to make this new company excel.

Then another company came into town. They promised me an even higher position and a piece of the pie, so I signed on with them. *Selfish ambition* means *always looking out for number one*. It's looking for a bigger reward. It's reaching for the next rung on the ladder of success. It's taking something away from someone else for your benefit. Selfish ambition never worries about who gets hurt, never sees the destruction that it leaves behind, never thinks about what someone else loses.

Like I said, I was not really acting like my father and, especially, not like my Heavenly Father. I was already a Christian when I did all of this. In the book of Proverbs it says, "An unfriendly man pursues selfish ends; he defies all sound judgment" (Prov. 18:1 NIV).

After seminary, when we returned to Tucson to start our church, one of the things I did was to go and make amends to the companies I had hurt or treated wrongly. I could not in good conscience do a work like this and not own up to the way I had treated these people. James tells us, "But if you harbor bitter envy and selfish ambition in your hearts, do not boast about it or deny the truth" (James 3:14 NIV).

The Philippians were in this same place. Some in the church were seeking their own way without any regard for others. Most churches in which we have served are the same. It's the Burger King mentality again. "I want it my way." I want the church service times my way. I want the music my way. I want the sermon my way. I want the Bible study my way. I WANT, I WANT, I WANT! That attitude doesn't work. It only hurts the body of Christ. James tells his people, "For where you have envy and selfish ambition, there you find disorder and every evil practice" (James 3:16 NIV).

Paul also addresses the issue of *vain conceit*. This is nothing more than empty boastfulness. Pride, arrogance or *"I am better than anyone else"* best describe this idea of *"vain conceit."* This is one character issue that I have had to deal with in the last few years. God has truly been gracious to me by giving me the ability to sing. I love to sing and I love how people respond to the music, but it was a problem early on.

Early in my life I would be asked to sing at revivals or church services. I was young and could play the guitar and I was, in my mind, the best. I loved the attention and the praise I was getting. My head was getting as big as Martin Short's head when he got stung by a bee in "Pure Luck." **"God really got something here when He saved me,"** I thought to myself. It has taken me years to really overcome that weakness.

I still sing and I still get complimented, but I know now that it's not what I have done, but what God has done through me. Maybe you are dealing with this character flaw as well. God has gifted you to do something in an amazing fashion. Don't forget, like I did, that it was God who began this good work in you. Thank Him for His generous gift to you.

Listen, just because we are Christians doesn't mean that we are automatically perfect. In the church there are a lot of imperfect Christian brothers and sisters. In God's family, there will be various differences, opposing political preferences, differing opinions, varied social concerns and what-not. It's really silly to think that just because we are joined as a church family, we won't have problems. We will. We are a family and, I suppose, we are normal.

Spiritual growth is not just coming to Jesus and by the wave of His hand we are perfected. We are commanded to grow in our spiritual walk. Paul tells the Philippians later in this chapter, "Continue to work out your salvation with fear and trembling" (2:12). Jesus tells us in Matthew, "Be perfect, even as your Father in heaven is perfect" (Matt. 5:48 NLT).

How are we to be perfect or how are we to grow in spiritual maturity? Paul says there has to be a transformation. There has to be this change taking place in our hearts. Paul says in 2 Corinthians, "But we all, with unveiled face, beholding as in a mirror the glory of the Lord, are being transformed into the same image from glory to glory, just as from the

Lord, the Spirit" (2 Cor. 3:18 NASB). An interesting word is used in this passage. The word for "transform" in the Greek carries the idea of "changing into."

If you have ever seen a monarch butterfly, you have seen its beautiful colors and grace, but its beginnings are quite unusual. The Monarch butterfly does not start out as a butterfly. It goes through a life-changing cycle. It begins as an egg, then a larva, and then it grows into a caterpillar. The caterpillar then spins a covering and in this covering is transformed into a butterfly. It has gone through the metamorphosis process.

Spiritual growth is focusing on Jesus, who He is, what He does, how He works and how He loves. As we focus our lives on Jesus, we are being changed. We are metamorphosing, as it were, from one level of glory to another level of glory, into His very image. Paul says later on in this letter, "I count all things to be loss in view of the surpassing value of knowing Christ Jesus my Lord" (Phil. 3:8 NASB).

I want us to discover how to grow spiritually and how we can have the character quality of *"selflessness."* The first thing we need to ask ourselves is, **Do we have that intimacy with Christ**? In other words, do we know and are we convinced that we are walking with Him? Once again Paul says, "If you have any encouragement from being united with Christ." If we are not in a close relationship with Him, then certainly we will not have that encouragement from our relationship with Jesus.

Growing in Christ comes from a deep and meaningful relationship with Him on a daily basis. We know that we are growing when we sense that whatever pleases Him pleases us. Whatever matters to Him matters to us. To say it another way, we see that our *selfish ambition* and *vain conceit* fades as our focus continues to be on Him. We not only look out for our own interests, but for the interests of others. We also hold others above ourselves. We recognize the value others have to God, to the church and to us. So, we find encouragement in our relationship with Jesus.

Let me ask another question, **Do we sense the comfort of His love?** Do we love other people? Do we see their value? Are we being more like Jesus? Becoming more like Jesus is realizing that we are commonly linked together as Paul says, "Being like-minded, having the same love, being one in spirit and purpose" (v.2 NIV).

Nothing grows love more than this idea of commonality or community. When we are willing to be like-minded (in the Greek the idea is "to have understanding"), when we grow in love toward each other, when we understand our purpose in what a Christian is and what a Christian does, then we enter into a relationship of unity or *"selflessness."* You see, when love inhabits the Christian life, there is no room to claim our own rights above another's. There is no place for our way to be the only way. Love joins us together to see the ultimate goal or purpose in living out the Christian life.

Then finally, we need to ask this question, *Do we really sense the fellowship of the Spirit?* Paul continues, "If any fellowship with the Spirit, if any tenderness and compassion" (v.1d). The Greek word for fellowship is one I'm sure you've heard. It's the word *"koinōnia."* This word is found 39 times in the New Testament. It can mean, "contribution, fellowship, participation, or sharing."

Let me put it this way. First I will state it negatively. *I know I am not in fellowship with the Spirit when I am out for myself and consider myself too important to be identified with any group or community of believers*. I hear that a lot. I know Christians who just flat out refuse to identify with a community of believers simply because they don't want to commit themselves to any one group. They want the best of everything without committing to anything.

This is nothing more than selfish ambition and vain conceit. When those two are present in the life of the believer then there is no room for *tenderness* and *compassion*. Christians who think they are too good to be a member of a church reject this notion of fellowship and participation. In other words, they refuse to be tender or show tenderness. The same can be said about compassion. Refusing to be a part of a community of believers displays a heart of pride. They think they're too good to contribute and too good to share.

Now, let me state this in a positive way. *I know I am in fellowship with the Spirit when I show tenderness and compassion to others*. Believers who truly commit their lives in a community with other believers have a compassionate heart and a tenderness of spirit. You see, the way people know that God has begun a good work in us is by believers displaying the workings of the Holy Spirit in the sphere of community.

Let's be honest, we all have a habit of hanging out with other sinners. Every Sunday we all sit in a building full of sinful people, but the only difference between us and those on the outside is that we are sinners saved by grace, growing in Christ-likeness together. We do that through fellowship with each other. Sharing what we have with each other. Contributing in different ways and by participating in the things that matter most. When we do these things, then we know that we are in fellowship with the Spirit. Ultimately this leads to encouragement in Christ, which leads to unity or *selflessness*.

This journey to joy is never easy. As a matter of fact, it's really down-right difficult. I think that is why many who say they are Christians simply give up. It's difficult for one reason—it goes against our very nature. This is not who we are. Listen to what Paul says here, "It wasn't so long ago that you were mired in that old stagnant life of sin. You let the world, which doesn't know the first thing about living, tell you how to live. You filled your lungs with polluted unbelief, and then exhaled disobedience. We all did it, all of us doing what we felt like doing, when we felt like doing it, all of us in the same boat. It's a wonder God didn't lose his temper and do away with the whole lot of us" (Eph. 2:1-3 MSG).

Now, I want to just say this before we go any further in this journey. The Word of God makes it very clear who we were before we entered into a relationship with Jesus. That is what Paul is saying in these verses to the Ephesians. This is who we were. This is not who we are, however, if we've entered into a relationship with Jesus. We cannot really expect to find joy on this journey if we are not changing from the inside out. Paul continues to say, "Instead, immense in mercy and with an incredible love, he embraced us. He took our sin-dead lives and made us alive in Christ. He did all this on his own, with no help from us!" (Eph. 2:4-5 MSG).

In essence he is saying that God loved us so much that He took the initiative to give us a way back to Him. He gave His life because of His love for us. He wants to remake us into His likeness. He wants to change us because, without this change, we cannot even attempt to live selfless lives.

If you are not sure about your relationship to Jesus Christ, then maybe right now, right where you are sitting, just open up your heart to Jesus. In a simple prayer confess that you are not a Christian, but would like to enter into that relationship with Him. You don't need to understand everything right up front. You just have to trust Him. Again Paul says, "Saving is all his idea, and all his work. All we do is trust him enough to let him do it. It's God's gift from start to finish!" (Eph. 2:8 MSG).

Maybe you are a Christian, but you know you haven't been living your life in the sphere of God's will. You may feel like a failure and think

God isn't really interested in you, but that is not true. I know how you feel and why you think that way. I have been there as well. Would you just ask God to forgive you? Would you ask Him to help you forgive yourself. It's easy to ask for forgiveness, but it's really hard to forgive yourself. I know about that, too.

I don't know where you are in your spiritual journey right now. I can only pray for God to guide you where He needs you to go. I would encourage you to find a fellowship of believers where you'll feel loved and wanted and that it will become your place of growth and service. This journey to joy is not exclusive, but inclusive.

> "God is building a home. He's using us all
> irrespective of how we got here
> in what he is building."
> (Ephesians 2:19 MSG)

# 8

# The Journey Through Humility
# Philippians 2:5-11

I remember years ago watching Muhammad Ali box. He was young and very confident of himself. He once said, *"I am the greatest, I said that even before I knew I was."* Anyone who has ever seen Muhammad Ali box could never deny that he in fact was one of the best. He knew it and so did the people he competed against. You might think he was arrogant and a braggart but what he said he did. He also said, *"It's hard to be humble, when you're as great as I am."*

Most of us have that problem. We think we're good at everything we touch or at least in most things. It is a problem I find myself dealing with at times. When I hear someone sing I think to myself *"I can do better than that."* Or when I hear someone give the message the thought pops into my head, *"I would have said it this way."* I may not be as loud vocally about it as Ali was but I'm not that much different than he was.

On this journey to joy, it is becoming increasingly obvious that who we are, what we do, and the attitude with which we face our everyday lives will matter. It will matter as we travel this journey. Either we will find it rewarding or we will find ourselves regretting it. We can't make this journey on our own. We can't even have the hope of completing this journey if we come to it in our power or by our own determination.

Here's the thing, before we can attempt to begin this journey, we have to enter through a certain gate. There is only one way to begin this journey and it has nothing to do with how great we are. Sometimes when we sing the hymn, "How Great Thou Art," we think the song was written for us. Ali may have thought that he was the greatest, but time will reveal who is and always will be the greatest.

Jesus said that there are two gates, a broad gate and a narrow gate. As we read Matthew 7:13 we find that Jesus describes both gates. He says there is a broad gate and a lot of people are going through it. It isn't restrictive. Anyone can go through it.

Everyone is headed on some journey. It could be the journey to self-fulfillment or material wealth. It could be for self enjoyment or physical ecstasy. It could be for living a good life or creating a prosperous business. Whatever the case may be, we are all on some journey, but the direction will determine the outcome of our journey. Jesus said that the broad gate leads to the broad way and in the end it leads to hopelessness or ruin. Why? Because through this broad gate and on this broad way there are no requirements. There are no restrictions. There are no commitments. It is come as you are, do what you want, live as you like and get all you can. You live with this same attitude, *"I am the greatest."*

The narrow gate, however, is very restrictive. You see, you can't take all your baggage with you. You can't determine what you will do or how you will do it. There's only one way to enter into it, only one way. The only way to enter is by acknowledging that you are willing to leave everything at that door. It means leaving self, leaving selfish desires, pride, arrogance, and this mentality, *"I am the greatest."*

Now, in order to enter in through this gate we need to make a decision. In fact we have to make this confession, *"Jesus Christ is Lord."* The secret to a maturing spiritual journey is making this confession. It is releasing my pride and arrogance and having my sins forgiven. It is ultimately letting go of running my life, of choosing my way, of using my own GPS and letting *"God begin a good work in me."*

This is where we find ourselves in this passage, journeying through the character of *humility*. Paul has just encouraged the Philippian believers to live in unity. He says that they were to demonstrate selflessness toward each other. If we say we are Christians, then our lives need to demonstrate that. Talk is cheap. We can say we are Christians, and there are many who swear they are, but their lives are devoid of any evidence.

So how do we know that we are Christians? How do we know that on this spiritual journey we are growing? Paul has just said that the evidence of a redeemed heart is one that demonstrates *selflessness* (Phil. 2:1-4). Then he adds this, "Have this attitude in yourselves which was also in Christ Jesus" (Phil. 2:5 NASB). Here it is, the ultimate proof that we are maturing on our spiritual journey, *Christ-likeness*. There can be no greater example of humility than Jesus Christ. The quest for character always begins and ends with Jesus. Paul's whole basis for Christian character is built around the person of Jesus Christ. Here he is reiterating what he has said in chapter one and verse six, "He who began a good work in you."

If we are to have this attitude, then we need to know something about the character of Jesus. So Paul begins to describe *humility* in the Christian life by using Jesus as the example. He says, "Have this attitude in yourselves which was also in Christ Jesus, who, although He existed in the form of God, did not regard equality with God a thing to be grasped" (2:5-6 NASB).

We cannot know anything about the Person of Jesus Christ until we make a conscience effort to search the Scriptures. The Word of God tells us who Jesus was and what He was like. The Scriptures tell us that He was indeed God, He is the creator of all things and He is the Light and Life for all men. "In the beginning was the Word, and the Word was with God, and the Word was God. He was in the beginning with God. All things came into being through Him, and apart from Him nothing came into being that has come into being. In Him was life, and the life was the Light of men. The Light shines in the darkness, and the darkness did not comprehend it" (John 1:1-5 NASB).

The Scriptures tell us that He came in the form of a man and that He was accessible. "And the Word became flesh, and dwelt among us . . . what we have heard, what we have seen with our eyes, what we have looked at and touched with our hands" (John 1:14; 1 John 1:1 NASB).

The Scriptures tell us that He was tempted in all things and is sympathetic towards us because of that. "For we do not have a high priest who cannot sympathize with our weaknesses, but One who has been tempted in all things as we are, yet without sin" (Hebrews 4:15 NASB).

So, when we come to this issue of humility, we need to see it in light of the person of Jesus Christ. This attitude is nothing more than Christ-likeness. It is being changed from one level of glory to another level of glory, into His very image. It is demonstrating that Jesus Christ truly lives within us.

Paul is not just concerned that we just have the right attitude. He also wants to make sure we understand why we should have this attitude. First he says that position should never take the place of purpose. Listen to what he says, "Although He existed in the form of God, did not regard equality with God a thing to be grasped" (v.6 NASB). I believe that here he is making a reference to those that had selfish ambitions and were prideful or full of vain conceit.

"Here is God" Paul says, "Here is the Almighty seeing the greater good or purpose." Here, Jesus is laying aside his rightful place of glory and honor for someone else. He stepped out of heaven and became human for you and me. There is no selfish ambition here. There is no pride or vain conceit with Him. He does it purely because of his love for us. He sees the need, He considers us, and while he still retains His position as God, He makes Himself to be a servant at the same time. Paul goes on to say, " . . . but emptied Himself, taking the form of a bond-servant, and being made in the likeness of men. Being found in appearance as a man, He humbled Himself by becoming obedient to the point of death, even death on a cross" (2:7-8 NASB).

Just because we are called upon to serve one another does not mean we lose ourselves in some lowly position. Servitude is not a denying of one's own ability, but the willingness to serve even when those abilities are not needed at that moment. Jesus did not cease to be God when he became human. He was very much God, but at the same time He was very much man.

This is where we have a tendency to get off the journey. We think that if we present ourselves as servants, that we will be overlooked for some greater position or opportunity. Somehow, others will not recognize that we are the preacher, the teacher, the deacon, the Chaplain, the soloist or the prayer warrior. We want the reward before the effort is even given. We want the recognition before we do the service. When we look at what Jesus did, it really should shame us for even thinking about ourselves first.

The Pharisees were religious people who loved attention and praise. Their every effort was done so that everyone could see them. Jesus said that they have already received their reward. The only thing about the praises of men is that one day you are a hero and the next day you become a zero. It doesn't last. True humility is seeking to please Jesus. With or without the recognition, we serve because of our relationship with Jesus Christ.

As Christian servants we need to be a light to a dying world. As we serve one another we are demonstrating the love and light of Jesus Christ. Jesus tells us, "Let your light so shine before men that they may see your moral excellence and your praiseworthy, noble, and good deeds and recognize and honor and praise and glorify your Father Who is in heaven" (Matthew 5:16 AMP).

As Christian servants we are to be accessible to a lost and dying world. The thing about being a monk is that they are never around other people. More specifically, they are never around lost people. Heaven forbid that a sinner brush up against them. But here we are and a person off the street comes and sits on OUR PEW and we rush off to the preacher to complain. We talk about reaching a lost and dying world, but that is all we intend to do. We like the country club we belong to. We have a long-time membership there. We don't like it when filthy, sinful people walk into our plush, sanitized havens.

Sometime after my wife and I arrived at the Brethren church and after evaluating what needed to be done, we created a ministry called **Bridge Builders**. This was designed to reach people who had really never been to church and for people whose lives were devastated by wrong choices. We had people living on the street, drug abusers, divorcees, and people just out of rehabilitation centers coming to worship.

One Sunday morning I saw an elderly lady sitting in **her** pew stewing. I walked over to her and said good morning and then asked what was happening in her life. She proceeded to tell me that she was mad at me. When I asked her why she said, *"You are bringing drug addicts, whores and dirty people into my church and I don't like it. This is my church."* "Funny," I said, *"I don't remember you hanging on the cross?"* Needless to say, she stopped coming altogether.

Listen to what James says, "My dear brothers and sisters, as believers in our glorious Lord Jesus Christ, never think some people are more important than others. Suppose someone comes into your church meeting wearing nice clothes and a gold ring. At the same time a poor person comes in wearing old, dirty clothes. You show special attention to the one wearing nice clothes and say, 'Please, sit here in this good seat.' But you say to the poor person, 'Stand over there,' or, 'Sit on the floor by my feet.' What are you doing? You are making some people more important than others, and with evil thoughts you are deciding that one person is better" (James 2:1-4 NCV).

Here's a second thing, as Christians we are set apart to do His service. When Paul uses these titles for Jesus, he does it for a reason. The name *Jesus* signifies His humanity. We talked about that just a moment ago. Jesus was all God and all man. Listen, we are all human. None of us has obtained perfection. We sin on a daily basis. The problem with most of us is we have this tendency to be farsighted when it concerns our sinfulness. Yet, when we see the sinfulness of others, well, then we have 20/20 vision. "And why worry about a speck in your friend's eye when you have a log in your own?" (Matt. 7:3 NLT).

Listen, as Christians, even though we are human, we are also spiritual. Paul says, "Don't you realize that your body is the temple of the Holy Spirit, who lives in you and was given to you by God?" (1 Cor. 6:19 NLT). Paul also tells the Galatian Christians, "If we live in the Spirit, let us also walk in the Spirit" (Gal. 5:25 NKJV).

So, if we continue to live for ourselves, could it be that maybe we are not in a relationship with Jesus? Could it be that we may be on the wrong road (the broad way), taking the wrong journey? Are we sure that we are following the right road map? Paul tells the Romans, "Those who are living by their natural inclinations have their minds on the things human nature desires; those who live in the Spirit have their minds on spiritual things" (Rom. 8:5 NJB).

Now the title of *"Christ"* carries the idea of *"Messiah"* or *"anointed One."* In the Old Testament whenever someone was anointed it meant that they were set apart to do a special work. Jesus Christ was set apart to do a work which only He could fulfill. Paul says that He was "obedient to the point of death, even the death on the cross" (2:8 NASB). This was His mission and purpose.

Now, God has not called any of us to sacrifice our lives in the manner that Jesus did. That requirement has been fulfilled, but he has set us apart for a specific reason. Peter says, "But you are a chosen people, a royal priesthood, a holy nation, a people belonging to God, that you may declare the praises of him who called you out of darkness into his wonderful light. Once you were not a people, but now you are the people of God; once you had not received mercy, but now you have received mercy" (1 Pet. 2:9-10 NIV).

Humility is acknowledging that we, "have been bought with a price" (1 Cor. 6:20 NASB). Humility is acknowledging we have been set apart for a specific task or purpose. Humility is acknowledging that we are here to serve and not be served. Humility is acknowledging that Jesus Christ is Lord.

Dr. John MacArthur wrote, "Our supreme calling is to serve God with all our being, first and foremost in worship. Through Christ, the writer of Hebrews tells us, we are to 'continually offer up a sacrifice of praise to God, that is, the fruit of lips that give thanks to His name' (Heb. 13:15). True worship includes many things besides the obvious ones of prayer, praise, and thanksgiving. It includes serving God by serving others in His name, especially fellow believers. Sacrificial worship includes 'doing good and sharing; for with such sacrifices God is pleased' (Heb. 13:15-16; cf. Phil. 4:14). But above all else, our supreme act of worship is to offer ourselves wholly and continually to the Lord as living sacrifices." (MacArthur, John F. The MacArthur New Testament Commentary, Romans 9-16, 1994 The Moody Bible Institute of Chicago. Database © 2008 WORDsearch Corp. MacArthur, pg 138)

Which leads me to this final thought, God will always reward His children. The title, *Lord,* carried the idea in the Old Testament of *God.* The Jews regarded the name of God so sacred that they used other terms to describe Him. One of the common terms they used was this term "Lord." Simply put, when you and I say "Jesus is Lord" we are saying Jesus is God.

In his encounters with the risen Christ, one of the disciples makes an astounding claim concerning Jesus. Thomas, having just been told that they had seen the risen Lord, still wanted proof, like many of us. Thomas says that, unless he sees with his own eyes and touches His wounds for himself, he would not believe. Then Jesus appears to Thomas and asks Him to do certain things. After that, Thomas makes this confession, **"Ho kurios mou kai ho theos mou."** Pretty impressive, huh? Literally it means, **"*The Lord of me, the God of me.*"** Jesus is not only Lord of all, He is God of all. If He is not Lord of all in your life, He cannot be God at all in your life.

Paul says once again, "For this reason also, God highly exalted Him, and bestowed on Him the name which is above every name" (2:9 NASB). What Jesus went through while on earth was nothing compared to what God would do for Him. His reward was not in the present, but in the eternal. He didn't look at what He had or what He had given up. He saw what was ahead on this journey to joy and He withstood the temporal suffering and lack of worship and anchored himself on the promise of God.

If you are looking for the praise and adoration of others as a Christian, then you have missed what a Christian is altogether. If you are serving right now, if you are counting on your own abilities, if you are bragging about your life's accomplishments, then you already have your reward. However, if you are doing the things God has called you to do, if you are serving, praying, helping, seeking, for the sake of Jesus, then anchor yourself to His promises, because God will always reward faithfulness.

"Then at last everyone will say, 'There truly is a reward for those who live for God; surely there is a God who judges justly here on earth'" (Ps. 58:11 NLT).

"The godly can look forward to a reward, while the wicked can expect only judgment" (Prov. 11:23 NLT).

"Remember that the Lord will reward each one of us for the good we do, whether we are slaves or free" (Eph. 6:8 NLT)

"Remember that the Lord will give you an inheritance as your reward, and that the Master you are serving is Christ" (Col. 3:24 NLT).

"So do not throw away this confident trust in the Lord. Remember the great reward it brings you!" (Heb.10:35 NLT).

"And remember that the heavenly Father to whom you pray has no favorites. He will judge or reward you according to what you do. So you must live in reverent fear of him during your time as "foreigners in the land" (1 Pet. 1:17 NLT).

God's reward to Jesus was that He would be given a name above every other name that, "at the name of Jesus every knee will bow, of those who are in heaven and on earth and under the earth, and that every tongue will confess that Jesus Christ is Lord, to the glory of God the Father" (2:10-11 NASB).

God rewards those who are faithful, as well. Faithfulness encompasses humility. John tells us, "To him who overcomes, to him I will give some of the hidden manna, and I will give him a white stone, and a new name written on the stone which no one knows but he who receives it." (Rev. 2:17 NASB).

So in this journey to joy don't be consumed by what you don't have or the recognition you don't get. Don't live selfishly, but selflessly. In humility exemplify the Lord you profess to believe in and worship.

Muhammad Ali believed with his whole heart he was the greatest. I am sure he stills feels same. But how do you measure greatness? The disciples asked this same question. Then Jesus responds by saying this, "Whoever then humbles himself as this child, he is the greatest in the kingdom of heaven." And then later on he says this, "But let the greatest among you be your servant" (Matt.18:1&4 NASB; Matt. 23:11 BBE)

> "Every knee will bow,
> every tongue confess,
> that Jesus Christ is Lord,
> to the glory of God the Father."
> (Phil. 2:10-11 NASB)

# 9

# The Journey Through Commitment
# Philippians 2:12-18

I had an overwhelming urge to embarrass myself one morning. I stood up on the bathroom scale, which my wife had recently bought, and decided to see where my weight was. It took me a few minutes to figure out how this thing worked. That should tell you how long it's been since I weighed myself.

As I got on, the thing kept scrolling, looking for those magic numbers. It was almost like those game show wheels where they spin it and it lands on some gift or amount of money. As the scale came to an abrupt halt, it gave me this flashing statement, "WOW!" I knew I was in trouble then. Well, not really, but what I saw was not a number I liked and I was sure my doctor would agree.

But it was not enough to just endure that humiliation. I also went in and took my blood pressure and, man, the numbers were something like 145 over *I'm going to die*! I made a decision right there to lose some weight. Also, I was going to try and get my blood pressure down before my doctor prescribed some kind of medication for it.

In the last few months I made a commitment to walk at least a mile and half a day. I get up put on my sweats and then head out to walk. Recently, I have begun to run short distances on my walks. It takes a big commitment. I am beginning to feel that maybe this was not such a good idea after all. I mean, it really takes a lot of work to hit that first stretch and it takes a bigger effort to go the last few feet. I have to admit, though, I have managed to lose several pounds in just a short time.

Physical exercise was not all that I needed, however. My diet had to change as well. I gave up eating at Wendy's and Whataburger. I gave up snacking on chips and my daily intake of the real thing, Coke. I have committed to eating cottage cheese, chicken and salads. I must confess that sometimes a hamburger really sounds good, but I can't give in just yet. Oh, I still drink a Coke now and then. I'm not sure about giving that up completely. I also cut back on drinking coffee to one day a week.

In this journey to joy we have to, of necessity, go through the character of commitment. Commitment is a requirement in almost anything we do in life. Commitment is necessary in relationships, raising children, having a job, buying a house, using credit cards and the likes. Without commitment there is no foundation upon which to build. Marriages fail simply because there is no real commitment to one another. People jump from job to job simply because they lack commitment. Even Christians fail because of a lack of commitment to any one body or to spiritual growth.

Paul knows that and he sees that the potential for these believers to give up is very real. He sees that without his presence or in the event of his death they could very well give up on the journey, give up on the fight, quit the race or just plain give up. When Paul made a commitment to Jesus on the road to Damascus, he kept it. He tells us, "I have fought the good fight, I have finished the race, and I have remained faithful" (2 Tim. 4:7 NLT).

Commitment is everything in the Christian life and without it, well, the journey will seem long and hard. Some of us have a tendency to give up as soon as we hit a speed bump or encounter a road block. Maybe that is where you're at right now. You feel that staying on this journey isn't really worth it. Let me just say this, don't give up! Look up and Jesus will help you through. The Bible tells us to, "Commit your actions to the Lord, and your plans will succeed" (Prov. 16:3 NLT).

Paul tells these Christians at Philippi, "So then, my beloved, just as you have always obeyed, not as in my presence only, but now much more in my absence, work out your salvation with fear and trembling; for it is God who is at work in you, both to will and to work for His good pleasure" (2:12-13 NASB).

I want us to understand something before we go any further. Commitment without obedience is really fruitless. Is that possible?

Certainly! I made a commitment to lose weight. As I said before, I walk a mile and a half a day and I make a conscious effort to consider what I eat. But let's say, I make a commitment to walking, but I keep on eating the wrong things. On the one hand, I am committed to physical activity but on the other hand I am being disobedient to physical nutrition. One without the other only produces frustration.

The same goes for the Christian life. Many Christians are committed to the church, but are disobedient to the Lord. Physically they are doing something, like serving in some capacity at church, tithing, or singing in the choir, but spiritually they are undisciplined or anemic. They have no power or purpose and eventually they give up their service and ultimately give up on the church. Doing something doesn't necessarily mean you are growing.

In this section Paul encourages these Christians as well as mildly commanding them to "work out your salvation with fear and trembling." There is a tendency here, to go too far into some doctrinal heresy. The working out of our salvation has been misunderstood by many well-meaning people. It has led many denominations to form a system of belief that compels them to **work for** rather than **work out** the reality of the gift of grace.

Paul introduces us to the reality of the Christian commitment by this phrase "so then." In other translations they use the words, "therefore" or "wherefore." It can mean "as a result of." Paul tells us, as a result of what we have just said concerning Christian behavior, work out your own salvation with fear and trembling. Paul says, "Jesus humbled himself and became obedient unto death, even death on the cross. Jesus showed the course of humility and obedience; therefore the Christian is to work out his or her salvation."

Here's the thing, as a community of believers we can do great things. We can encourage each other, help each other and pray for each other. As a community of believers we need to be mindful of one another, treating each other with respect, and showing humility towards one another.

Paul now turns his focus from community to personal. To live the Christian life in the presence of other believers is easy. It's easy to be a Christian when you are around the preacher, but what if, all of a sudden, you had to go through some unexpected circumstance? Would you still be as faithful? Paul says that no matter what happens these Philippian Christians were to continue in the Christian faith through conduct and character.

Nothing brings to light the authenticity of our Christianity than unexpected circumstances. This is where we find that struggle to either continue or give up. It could be a favorite pastor leaving after so many years. It could be a spouse or a parent dying. It could be a transfer from a job or even the loss of a job. When these things take place, our faith is put to the test.

In any event, Paul encourages these Christians and we can include ourselves, to continue to *work out our salvation*. So what does he mean? Well, I want to be very clear here that Paul is not saying we need to work for our salvation. He has already told us in the first chapter, that it is God who has begun a good work. He knows that salvation is from God. Nothing you and I do will ever earn us our salvation.

Salvation is by grace. It is God's gift to the sinner. We cannot work for it or earn it or buy our way. We must accept it and then live it. The epistle of James is a very practical guide to all believers. It shows us how to work out our salvation. Studying this epistle will show us the true characteristics of believers. We see things like accepting all people and not judging, being grateful in hard circumstances, giving rather than taking, sharing rather than hoarding, holding our tongues instead of blistering someone with them. We see the fruit of the Spirit displayed in a life that has been redeemed. In reality, it is the characteristics of humility and obedience, conduct and character in the making.

Paul tells the Galatian Christians, "But the fruit of the Spirit is love, joy, peace, patience, kindness, goodness, faithfulness, gentleness and self-control . . . Since we live by the Spirit, let us keep in step with the Spirit" (Gal. 5:22-26 NIV). He goes on to say to the Christians at Ephesus, "Therefore do not be foolish, but understand what the Lord's will is . . . be filled with the Spirit . . . Submit to one another out of reverence for Christ" (Eph. 5:17-21 NIV).

The idea of working out our salvation does not mean we have to do something to earn it. This is what Paul means by "working out our salvation." He says that salvation requires an active role from us. We can't just sit back with the mentality, *"Let go and let God."* But that's what a lot of Christians are content to do. They simply believe that God is responsible for growing them. God is responsible for keeping them safe from sin.

Nothing is more dangerous than a Christian who is passive in their belief. This is why some who call themselves Christians give up midway through the journey. They have no discipline and no commitment. They have a misconception that God is supposed to see them through, keep them safe, keep them warm and fed and, if not, then they think He doesn't care or isn't really concerned.

The Bible shows us that we must be engaged in our spiritual growth. In the Gospel of Luke, Jesus tells us, "Strive to enter in at the strait gate" (Luke 13:24 KJV). Paul says that, "I strive always to keep my conscience clear before God and man" (Acts 24:16 NIV). He goes on to say to the Corinthians, "but I discipline my body and make it my slave" (1 Cor. 9:27 NASB). And to Timothy he says, " . . . discipline yourself for the purpose of godliness" (1 Timothy 4:7 NASB).

Spiritual growth, like exercise, takes an effort on our part. We can say that we believe in physical fitness, but if all we do is stand on the treadmill without turning it on, who are we kidding? If we have a bunch of workout videos and never put them in the DVD player, who are we kidding? Yet, that is what a lot of Christians do, they have the equipment and instructions, but they don't have the discipline or commitment to turn the thing on. God began a good work in us. He has given us what we need in order to grow, but it will not happen if we just stand there and don't tap into His power.

So how do we, in simple terms, *work out* our salvation? Well, first we commit ourselves completely to God. Paul has given us the example of Jesus in the previous verses (5-11). Jesus was faithful to all God had called Him to do including the journey to the cross. Regardless of what God calls us to do, we should be completely anchored to Him.

Second, I need to commit to avoiding sinful passions. Paul says, "Do all things without grumbling or disputing" (v.14). You and I both know full well the things that seem to attract our attention rather quickly. The devil knows our weaknesses and don't think for a moment he won't exploit them. The Apostle John tells us, "Do not love the world nor the things in the world" (1 John 2:15 NASB).

Some of us like to grumble or say things under our breath because we disagree with something. We like to complain simply because it's not the way we want things to go, like the senior adult lady at the Brethren church. That's what Paul meant when he used the word *grumbling*. He meant complaining.

We are not only prone to complain, but we love to share our *opinions*. Man! Do I love to share my opinions. One member of a church told me I was opinionated. I told her that I had to be in order to keep up with her. *Disputing* means, *arguments* or *doubting*. When I am opinionated, I doubt the ability of someone else. This usually means that I doubt that God can handle the situation.

A third way to work out my salvation is I commit to reading God's Word daily. I'm not talking about giving a token five minutes by reading something and then rushing off not remembering what we have read. I am talking about sitting down and reading His Word with the intent of learning and growing through some spiritual truth we have gained. It means we study it, struggle with it and then live it. Peter said, "like newborn babies, long for the pure milk of the word, so that by it you may grow in respect to salvation" (1 Pet. 2:2 NASB).

Paul says we are to, "hold fast the word of life" (v.16). That means we have a firm grasp on its truth and the power it has to liberate a sinful person or sinful persuasions. This is not merely to look good or be good. We are not just to live moral lives. All that is good, but here the understanding is that we show why we are living this kind of life. And the reason is simply because of the Word of life.

We are new creations, not because of what we do, or the way we act, or the fact that we refrain from certain things. We are new creations because of what He has done and is doing in our lives. So the more we commit to reading and studying His Word, the more we are changed. The more we study, the more we realize that we are sinful and need His grace and His cleansing day by day.

The fourth thing is we commit ourselves to prayer. We pray for an increasing knowledge of God. We pray for guidance and for His leading. We pray for understanding even in times of uncertainty. We pray for vision, opportunities and for safety. Paul tells the Ephesians, "With all prayer and petition pray at all times in the Spirit, and with this in view, be on the alert with all perseverance and petition for all the saints" (Eph. 6:18 NASB).

But here is a greater reason to make this commitment to take this journey. In this journey to joy we are not left on our own. We are not on this journey wondering if we are doing the right thing or going the right way. God always has a part in all that He begins. Paul says, "Work out your salvation with fear and trembling; for it is God who is at work in you, both to will and to work for His good pleasure" (2:12-13 NASB).

Listen, God began a good work in us when we came to know Christ and accepted His gift of grace. Paul says that God who has done this, will also complete it. In other words, God is working within us, in our hearts, prompting us, guiding us to do the things that please Him. Has it ever occurred to you why you love going to church? Has it ever entered your mind why you like serving in the homeless ministry or children's services, in the choir or in just maintaining the facilities?

It is the Spirit of God that prompts us to refrain from complaining and being overly opinionated. It is God's Holy Spirit that causes us to love one another, serve one another and pray for each other. It is God's Spirit working deep within our hearts to show mercy, compassion, keep the unity in peace and to avoid vain conceit and selfish ambitions. It is God working to complete what He has begun.

It is God who is at work in us. It is His ever-present Holy Spirit that resides in us and continues to change us into the very likeness of Christ. Nothing is more awesome, more thought inspiring than this doctrine of sanctification. It is God working in us.

If this is true, then why is the Christian church, and more specifically the Christian, so powerless in our world today? Why is it that we don't have that same passion or seem to lose our way from time to time? Why don't we hunger and thirst after righteousness? Well, it really comes down to this statement, "Work out your salvation with *fear* and *trembling*.

Paul is not stating here that we should fear losing our salvation. Nothing can be more hazardous to the living Christian life than to believe that we are in danger of losing our salvation if we fall into sin for some reason. God has begun a good work in us, and He intends to continue that work. If this is true, then, certainly He is able to keep that which we committed to Him until the return of Christ or our exit from this world.

The reference here to fear and trembling can best be understood as *being serious about the Christian life*. I believe this is another reason why many so-called Christians give up on the journey. They are not serious about their new life. They don't see the real value in being a new creation. They have, in essence, lost the wonder and reverence of God. God is the Father of Lights. God is light and in Him there is no darkness. They should be fearful if they lose that awe of God.

We should also be serious about our Christian life because in this life, the world will be opposed to us if we truly seek to live the Christian life. It will seek to undermine God's glorious message, as well as His messengers. We should always be aware of what the world is like. Jesus told His disciples that they should not be surprised if the world hated them. Why? Because the world hated Jesus then and it continues to this day. John said, "that the whole world lies in the power of the evil one" (1 John 5:19 NASB).

We should also be serious about our Christian life because of the people we are. Nothing good dwells in us and, when we realize that, we avoid any circumstance that may discredit our witness. That is what Paul meant when he said, "But I discipline my body and make it my slave, so that, after I have preached to others, I myself will not be disqualified" (1 Cor. 9:27 NASB).

When we enter through the narrow gate and commit to the journey on the narrow way, we don't do it because it keeps us out of hell. That is one good reason, but it isn't the only reason. As we have seen in the previous verses, we do it because that is what Jesus Christ did. He committed His life totally to the will and purpose of God. We do it because Jesus willingly gave His life for us. We do it because we believe that we are His children and have an eternal hope. We live our Christian lives in respect to that. In other words, we don't spend our time on foolishness. We also do it because we will face the discipline of God if we don't live in fear and trembling (cf. Hebrews 12).

I mentioned at the beginning that I had committed to walking and running. On the path where I run are some benches set several feet apart. I imagine that the person who designed the path envisioned times when people needed to stop and rest for a few minutes. In this journey to joy I believe that God has also designed periods in our lives for rest. They may come in a variety of forms, but however God designs these periods of rest, He does it for our spiritual health. The Bible tells us, "Rest in the Lord and wait patiently for Him" (Ps. 37:7 NASB). While we are resting I want us to consider the outcome of our willingness to stay committed to the Christian life.

First, when we are committed to the will and purpose of God, we acknowledge that we truly are children of God. "So that you will prove yourselves to be blameless and innocent, children of God above reproach" (v.15a).

Second, when we are committed to the will and purpose of God, we exemplify the God we serve to the lost world. "In the midst of a crooked and perverse generation, among whom you appear as lights in the world" (v.15b).

Finally, when we are committed to the will and purpose of God, suffering will not be a hindrance but a joy. "But even if I am being poured out as a drink offering upon the sacrifice and service of your faith, I rejoice and share my joy with you all. You too, I urge you, rejoice in the same way and share your joy with me." (vs.17-18).

> "Don't look for shortcuts to God . . .
> The way to lifeCto God!Cis vigorous
> and requires total attention."
> (Matt. 7:13 &14 MSG)

# 10

# The Journey Through Loyalty
# Philippians 2:19-24

Who would you say is your best friend? If you had to choose from the countless friends you have right now, who would you identify as your best friend? Friendships are very valuable. People who claim to have no friends lead a very lonely life.

Some of my pastor friends say their wives are their best friend. I'm sure Job, the Old Testament saint, would disagree with that. I've heard from our church people that their best friend is their dog or cat. I could see why they would say that, but my cat would only listen up to a point and then either close his eyes as if to say "boring" or just walk away and chase the birds, which were probably more interesting.

Throughout my years I have had several people I would call best friends. Two in particular come to mind. Larry, who I have mentioned at the beginning of this book, and Julio, someone I knew from grade school on up. I have never met anyone I could not be friends with. I have known a few who began as friends, but wound up really never talking with each other again.

Julio and I became friends sometime in grade school and we continued on to adulthood. He was my best friend and we did a lot of things together. When we entered Jr. High, that first year, we had a falling out. Every time he saw me he would use obscenities or punch me or anything he could to harass me. I remember one time, at school, screaming all kinds of obscenities at each other. Towards the end of that first year we made up and stayed friends all through the rest of our school days.

I never knew what happened to cause him treat me that way. When I asked him, he just said it didn't matter anymore. We remained friends well into our adult years. I attended his wedding and he did the same for me. Just after high school, I became a Christian, but he didn't and our lives seemed to take different paths. We were still friends, but not as close as we once were. The years slipped away and we grew further apart.

Julio and his wife divorced after his son was born. He moved back with his parents, and as far as I knew, he was still living with them. I hadn't seen him for a quite some time and after I returned from seminary we ran into each other again. We talked for a while, but our lives were just not the same. Just recently, I went by the place where he used to live only to find a "for sale" sign on the property.

As for Larry and me, well, we have a long history together as well. He is a Christian and was considered one of the fastest runners at the University of Arizona. I know because he reminds me of it even now. We met at the Baptist Student Center (*that's what it was called back in the old days*). We spent our time playing volleyball, foosball, chasing girls and going to class, usually in that order. Larry is the kind of person who is very sure of himself and is actually a very hard worker. When he graduated from college he took a job with Walsh Brothers and did very well. Later, he started his own business and continues to this day.

After college we went our separate ways. When my wife took the financial secretary's job at First Southern Baptist Church, she ran into Larry. We connected again and continued our friendship. I have worked with Larry for many years off and on. He gave me a job before we left for seminary. When I returned to start our church, we got together from time to time. Occasionally, I would go out on jobs with him just to break the never-ending cycle of the pastorate. He needed the help and I welcomed the break.

Even now, we still help each other out. He has helped me with worship and getting the right equipment for the church. When I needed help in setting up sound systems for people like David Meece, he came and took care of that. So, whenever he had a big job and needed extra help I would go and help him. We once spent three weeks at Homeland Security setting up nine auditoriums with audio/visual equipment. There isn't anything we wouldn't do for each other.

Though we don't always see eye to eye on things, we always know we are friends. When I went through some dark times in my ministry, Larry was there. He never tried to outguess the situation like Job's friends and he has never been critical of some of my ministry choices either. Larry just listens, not like Indy, my cat, who would just walk away and meow so I would let him out quickly.

Loyalty is a very rare commodity. You hardly see it, but when you do, when you experience it, it is one of the most beautiful moments in life. Abraham Lincoln once said, "I am a success today because I had a friend who believed in me and I didn't have the heart to let him down . . ." Again he says, "A friend is someone who understands your past, believes in your future, and accepts you just the way you are."

Paul had many friends and partners in his journey to joy. There was Barnabas, Erastus, Silas, Aquila and Priscilla to name a few. There was Mark, with whom he had a disagreement and refused to take him on a missionary journey early in his ministry. Paul was not perfect. He had his moments. Later in life Mark became one of Paul's disciples, but none had as close a relationship to him as Timothy.

So who was Timothy? Timothy was born to parents from different religious backgrounds. His mother was Jewish and his father was a Greek. Timothy was instructed by his mother and grandmother in the Jewish faith. Paul says of Timothy, "For I am mindful of the sincere faith within you, which first dwelt in your grandmother Lois and your mother Eunice, and I am sure that it is in you as well . . . and that from childhood you have known the sacred writings which are able to give you the wisdom that leads to salvation through faith which is in Christ Jesus" (2 Tim. 1:5 & 3:15 NASB).

Timothy was probably converted during Paul's first visit to Lystra and probably grew in his spiritual faith being instructed by the elders who were appointed to oversee the churches there. He isn't mentioned again until Paul's second visit there. He is thought by some to have had a particular calling, namely to be a missionary. Paul says, "Do not neglect your gift, which was given you through a prophetic message when the body of elders laid their hands on you" (1 Tim. 4:14 NIV).

Paul enjoyed Timothy's friendship, love and loyalty. He journeyed with Timothy on numerous occasions and, at times, left him in certain areas where he could continue the work. In one of Paul's letter to Timothy, he shares the connection they had with each other. Paul writes, "To Timothy, my dear son . . . I thank God, whom I serve . . . as night and day I constantly remember you in my prayers. Recalling your tears, I long to see you, so that I may be filled with joy. I have been reminded of your sincere faith, which first lived in your grandmother Lois and in your mother Eunice and, I am persuaded, now lives in you also. For this reason I remind you to fan into flame the gift of God, which is in you through the laying on of my hands. For God did not give us a spirit of timidity, but a spirit of power, of love and of self-discipline" ( 2 Tim. 1:2-7 NIV).

So, in our journey there are some we are more intimate with than others. I hope you have a group of people who you can count on, share with, and minister to in your walk of life. Paul had several, but some were closer than others.

Timothy was Paul's most loyal friend. What is loyalty and how do we define it? First to be loyal is to be **trustworthy.** Paul had an immeasurable confidence in Timothy. He says of him, "Timothy has proved himself, because as a son with his father he has served with me in the work of the gospel" (2:22 NIV). Timothy could be counted on no matter what the task. When the new churches needed shepherding, Timothy was entrusted with that work. When heresies arose, Paul had confidence in Timothy that he would know what to do to overcome those situations.

In his spiritual journey, Timothy was tested in many ways. In his upbringing, his conversion and in his leadership, he had proven to be trustworthy. That's why Paul could say, "I hope in the Lord Jesus to send Timothy to you soon, that I also may be cheered when I receive news about you. I have no one else like him" (2:19-20 NIV). He had a heart like Paul.

In our spiritual journey, we will be tested—you can count on that. But how we endure that test will be the result of whether we are truly a work of God or just a facade that we have draped over ourselves. We cannot be loyal to God and loyal to the world. In this life we need to make some hard decisions. Do we please the world, ourselves or those around us? Do we seek to please the Lord even if that includes suffering for Him? During Jesus' ministry here, many stopped following Him simply because they could not understand His teachings on eternal life. He even asked his closest disciples, "You do not want to go away also, do you?" (John 6:67 NASB).

Have you ever wanted to just walk away from Jesus? Have you ever in your spiritual journey wanted to just give up and let things in your life go back to the way they were? There have been times I was so frustrated about things that I just wanted to give it all up. A few years back I did just that, gave up. I lost myself at Sam's Club. The only problem was people soon found out that I had been a pastor before coming there.

By the way, we can't hide from God. He always knows where we're at. He knew where I was and He knew just how long He would leave me there. God knows where you're at as well. He sees you and he knows just exactly how long he will leave you there.

Loyalty is being dependable even when we don't understand God's leading. Loyalty is being committed even when we endure hardship. Loyalty is being faithful when we can't see the reasons why. The Bible tells us, "He who pursues righteousness and loyalty finds life, righteousness and honor" (Prov. 21:21 NASB).

As I mentioned before, I served the local Brethren church for three years. God called me out of Sam's Club to go and minister to this church. I asked, "Why?" but He just said,

Go." As a Southern Baptist I didn't want to jeopardize my opportunities in Southern Baptist work. But I went trusting, even though I couldn't honestly understand why. Even as I write, I still don't have a reason or purpose. I do have peace about it and I'm sure one day He will let me know the reason why. I just need to trust Him.

A second characteristic of loyalty is **genuineness**. Paul had complete confidence in Timothy because Timothy was genuine. Paul says, "I have no one else like him, who takes a genuine interest in your welfare. For everyone looks out for his own interests, not those of Jesus Christ" (2:20-21 NIV). Paul says that Timothy was the real McCoy. He had undisputed credibility.

Timothy exemplified true selflessness. Paul says that he had a real interest in people. He was not just out there for show. He wasn't trying to impress Paul. He wasn't seeking some kind of special recognition from the Philippian Christians. Timothy truly cared about the church.

Here is the secret to being genuine, "Serve wholeheartedly, as if you were serving the Lord, not men" (Eph. 6:7 NIV). We are to minister, serve, help or whatever else God calls us to do without selfish motives. Too many times when we do something "spiritual" we want everyone to know. We like to brag about how much we give, how much we do around the church, how many people we visit or hand out gospel tracts to. It's like being at the harbor where all the ships are blowing their horns to let you know they are coming in to dock.

Finally, loyalty is **commitment.** Paul says, "He (Timothy) has served with me" (v.22). No matter where Timothy was sent, he served. Even if Paul was not there, he served. Even when he wanted Paul to stay with him, he served. Even when he suffered for a period of time, he served. Timothy served not because he was making a good show for Paul, but because of Jesus Christ. Paul said that while others are seeking recognition for themselves, Timothy is serving for the sake of Christ.

Are you a loyal friend? While attending the BSU, a young lady approached me and asked if I would be willing to go and witness to her brother. I said, "Sure." It was easy to say in front of a lot of Christians. In essence, I was saying, "I must be really spiritual for people to come and ask **ME** to witness to their family." Talk is cheap. A few weeks later this woman's brother stopped to help someone with a flat tire on the freeway. As he was getting the tire out of the trunk, a car smashed into his and pinned him against the car in front. He died that night. Did he know Jesus? I don't know. I never acted on my words. Loyalty is love in action.

Are you a loyal friend? Remember, it isn't who sees you or who asks you or who notices what you do. It's whether you want to please Jesus or please yourself.

> "Loyalty makes a person attractive . . .
> Worship and obey the Lord your God
> with fear and trembling,
> and promise that you will be loyal to him."
> (Prov.19:22 NLT; Deut. 6:13 CEV)

# 11

# The Journey Through Persistence
# Philippians 2:25-30

Joe Montana was of the greatest quarterbacks ever to grace the football field. I have always been amazed at his persistence to get the ball clear down the football field. He was very successful in fourth quarter comebacks. Here was a young man who no one ever thought would amount to anything in the NFL. Today, however, when you speak of great quarterbacks, Joe Montana is at the top of the list.

I'm also reminded of a special friend who has spent most of her life on the mission field. Her persistence in her place of service is most extraordinary. Even when she encountered a sickness that could have ended her life, she continued serving on the mission field. She will probably never be mentioned in many mission news articles. Not many people will hear her name, yet, while serving in obscurity, she has made a huge impact. God knows who she is even though most will never know her. Her name is Denise Dunscomb.

To be successful you don't have to be someone of prominence, just persistent. You may not get the attention of the evening news, but if you are a servant of God, He makes a big deal out of it. If you are serving in a church out in some remote community I am sure a lot of people will never hear of it. I am sure that God has heard of your efforts, though, and He thanks you by blessing your ministry. The Bible tells us, "God watches where people go; he sees every step they take" (Job 34:21 NCV).

That describes Epaphroditus—someone who was unknown to most people, including most of us. Not much is said or known about him. All we know is what Paul says about him, "My brother and fellow worker and fellow soldier, who is also your messenger and minister to my need" (2:25 NASB).

If you are struggling along your journey with being noticed or having someone acknowledge that you exist, don't lose heart. We all crave recognition. We all want to be needed and wanted. We all desire to know that we matter, but God knows who we are even if the rest of the world may never hear of us. He not only knows us, but loves us.

On this journey, if our lives are never heard of, that's okay. It really isn't so much about who knows me as it is about what difference I make in someone else's life. There are a lot of things I have done in the past that I would certainly hope people would forget. But there are also the good things I have done and didn't really know I had done them.

Not long after we arrived in Texas to attend seminary, I received a call from a friend of ours. She said that as she was listening to the Christian radio station that day, she heard a young lady give her testimony. She didn't really catch everything she was talking about or her name but as this woman was concluding her conversation, our friend heard these words: *"I don't know where he's at now, but I want to thank Dave Gutierrez, because if it wasn't for him I would not be here sharing this with you today."*

Wow! I was speechless. I kept asking who this person was but our friend did not catch her name. I must confess that it could have been another person with this same name but if it wasn't, here was someone whose life was changed and I had something to do with it even though I do not know what, when or even where.

But it doesn't matter does it? As we journey through life we will touch people one way or another. We may know about it or maybe never know. Does it matter how we live then? Of course it does. It matters how we live not only in public, but also in private. Remember, "God watches where people go; he sees every step they take."

So how do we stay persistent in this journey to joy? How do we maintain our spiritual growth in an ever-changing world? First, let me say that persistence is not the same as pulling yourself up by your bootstraps. It isn't this attitude, *"I am going to get through this even if it kills me."* Persistence is not me putting all my might behind the effort.

Persistence is realizing what our weaknesses are and trusting in God to give us the strength to overcome those weaknesses. Persistence is doing the right thing even when we'd rather not. The writer of Hebrews says, "Therefore, since we are surrounded by such a great cloud of witnesses, let us throw off everything that hinders and the sin that so easily entangles, and let us run with perseverance the race marked out for us" (Heb. 12:1 NIV). This was Epaphroditus.

Paul says that Epaphroditus was a *"brother."* In the New Living Translation it says he was a *"true brother."* Brothers are funny people. If you've ever had a brother, you know they can be obnoxious, pushy, boastful or annoying. I should know, I have six of these creatures. But even though they may be these things, they are also protective, generous, helpful and good listeners.

This was really an enormous praise of Epaphroditus. For a guy that came out of nowhere, Paul really heaps on the praise. I have had good Christian friends who were like brothers to me. They would do anything for me. They listened and helped whenever I needed them. They stood by my side when there was a death in my family. They have at times corrected me when I was going in the wrong direction. That is what a family should do for one another.

So when Paul uses the word *"brother"* he is basically saying that there was an intimacy between them. I am sure that every moment they were with each other wasn't all peaches and cream. Paul I'm sure had his moments and I would guess so did Epaphroditus. We can't really appreciate family intimacy without experiencing some difficulties.

In our churches we need to have this family intimacy more and more. But I am a realist and I realize it isn't that way most of the time. We do have our pet peeves. We do like certain things our way. We certainly like to be the top dog in the pound. But there are those who have a genuine heart for the ministry. They are the silent ones. They are the ones who work behind the scenes. They are the ones most don't really see or know about.

Epaphroditus was a very humble and compassionate man. It says when he heard that the Philippian Christians were concerned about him he "was very distressed that you heard he was ill" (2:26 NLT). He was disturbed by this. He didn't want to add sorrow upon sorrow. As we said before, these Christians were heartbroken that Paul might be put to death. So Epaphroditus didn't want to add to that. As a matter of fact, they probably didn't know how sick he really was. Paul tells them that he almost died.

Paul also describes Epaphroditus as a *"fellow worker."* This guy is not only identified as a brother, but also as someone who is contributing to the ministry. I can just see him out there doing whatever work needed to be done even though he is sick. He isn't complaining he is just working. Once again, Paul says he just isn't a worker but a fellow worker. He is saying they have an intimacy that is continually growing as they continue to do the work together.

Paul also calls Epaphroditus, *"a fellow soldier."* What does he mean by soldier? Well, we all know that soldiers are men and women who have trained for combat. They study tactical maneuvers of the enemy. They learn to endure hardship. They are familiar with using a weapon or weapons of different kinds. They even learn how to watch each other's back. A soldier is one who follows orders and works within the sphere of submission to those in higher ranks.

This man, Epaphroditus, was well-trained in the truth. He knew how to spot the enemy or false doctrine. He learned how to handle the truth and how to endure hardship because of it. He was also submissive to Paul and his leadership. You might even say that Epaphroditus had Paul's back. That is why Paul calls him a *fellow worker* and a *fellow soldier*. Paul says, "Suffer hardship with me, as a good soldier of Christ Jesus. No soldier in active service entangles himself in the affairs of everyday life, so that he may please the one who enlisted him as a soldier" (2 Tim. 2:3-4 NASB).

Then finally, we come to the last two things Paul says about him. Paul says that Epaphroditus was a *"messenger"* and a *"minister."* The Philippians longed to help Paul in his ministry but had not had another opportunity (v.30). Epaphroditus took on the mission of making sure Paul received this gift. In the process Paul says that Epaphroditus risked his life doing so (v.30).

The gift these Christians sent by the hand of Epaphroditus was apparently more than enough. Paul says in Philippians 4:18 that he was lacking nothing because of this sacrificial gift. Through the hands of Epaphroditus the Philippian Christians ministered to Paul. I think when Paul says that Epaphroditus ministered to his need it was in reference to the gift that these Christians had sacrificially given.

Let me say this one last thing in closing. Paul expresses a profound heart of gratitude. Paul is a very compassionate man for he is not the man that he once was. Previous to his conversion experience, he was callous and indifferent to the Christian way. Murdering people or attacking the young Christian church was not only a religious mandate for him but a protection of the old ways.

How many times have we caused more harm in the church because of our insistence on the old ways? How many times have churches split because one group or another group wanted it their own way? How many times has the Christian church been hurt because Christians refuse to submit to God? Well, there have been countless times this has happened in the church through the years.

Before his conversion, Paul was no different. In the final verses of this chapter we see a different and changed heart. He says he was sending Epaphroditus back, "because he was longing for you all" (v.26). He saw that Epaphroditus was homesick and he understood that his home church could minister to him better than he could. Paul goes on to say, "Therefore I have sent him all the more eagerly so that when you see him again you may rejoice and I may be less concerned about you" (v.28 NASB).

Not only does he display compassion, but gratitude. First, he is thankful to God that Epaphroditus had regained his health. Second, he is thankful that God had not laid a deeper burden on his heart, that being the death of Epaphroditus if God had not healed him. Being in prison was a very uncomfortable experience, but the death of a loved one, or in this case a fellow Christian, would be more than he could handle (v.27). So he is grateful for God's ever-watchful eye on his situation.

Then finally, the evidence of Paul's change of heart is the respect he has for Epaphroditus. He says, "Receive him then in the Lord with all joy, and hold men like him in high regard" (v.29). In other words, he is saying that men like him have proven their worth by their character and their commitment to the Lord's work. It goes along with what he said previously, " . . . with humility of mind regard one another as more important than yourselves" (v.3).

From obscurity to prominence. From a nobody to a somebody. Every one of us, whether we are in the limelight or in the shadows, in the eyes of the Lord is prominent. Job says once again, "God watches where people go; he sees every step they take."

I began this with the idea of persistence. Why? Because it takes persistence to continue to serve the Lord as we travel on this journey. It takes persistence to continue to be a *brother* or *sister* in the Lord when we disagree with each other. It takes persistence to do the right thing rather than things that could harm the church or other people. It takes persistence to continue to be a *fellow worker* when it seems we are the only one that seems to care for the church and its ministries.

It takes persistence to continue to be a *fellow soldier*, fighting this good fight, even when a crisis occurs, when our health seems to consume us or the world around us is really taking the fight to us. It takes persistence to continue to bring the *message* when no one seems to be listening. It takes persistence to continue to *minister* when others don't seem to notice our efforts or show gratitude for it.

I mentioned Denise, a missionary friend of ours. She would best exemplify the Epaphroditus character. This woman has dedicated her life to serving others in a country that is very volatile. She risks the possibility of contracting some disease, but continues to put others before her own physical needs and keeps on praying for those of us she has left behind in America. This journey to joy will take daily persistence. Paul encourages the Galatian Christians by telling them, "And let us not get tired of doing what is right, for after a while we will reap a harvest of blessing if we don't get discouraged and give up" (Gal. 6:9 TLB).

God is always looking out for His children. He sees and knows what we do, what we are going through and what He needs to do to help us along. You and I are never alone and we are never to give up the fight. That is why Paul tells these Galatian Christians not to get tired of doing what is right. God will bless in His time.

> "Be strong and courageous, and do the work.
> Don't be afraid or discouraged,
> for the Lord God, my God, is with you.
> He will not fail you or forsake you . . ."
> (1 Chronicles 28:2 NLT)

# 12

# Conclusion

We were more than three quarters of the way home from Del Rio, Texas, when the traffic suddenly came to a slow pace and all of us began to merge into one lane. As we were nearing the Arizona border, we had to stop at the border checkpoint. Each car had to acknowledge the authority of the officer asking questions and looking in and around the cars and trucks. I suppose they do this hoping to prevent harm to American citizens or people in general. It is a preventative measure to avoid the tragedy of 9/11.

With that in mind, this is where we are in our journey to joy, half way. We are here at this checkpoint right now to make sure that we do not have anything that could potentially harm others or ourselves. God the Father has brought us to this place to make sure it is safe to continue on.

As we journey on this road it is becoming quite clear that right conduct leads to godly character and godly character leads to right conduct. We said that we can know that God has truly begun a work in us by the character being produced in us. That character then is manifested in our everyday conduct.

All the things we have talked about thus far complement each other. Servitude is the outward expression of selflessness. When we demonstrate humility, it reveals the confidence we have that it is God who has begun this good work in us and it has nothing to do with self-effort. When we demonstrate a heart of love for others, God and ministry, we make a commitment to spiritual unity. When we display an attitude of gratitude, loyalty springs forth. When we are persistent in pleasing Jesus, our decisions will reflect the right thing to do.

It is truly important that we understand that the Christian life is not one where we make the rules. God has already put forth His plan for eternal life. Our decision is either to follow His way or try and find our own way. It is equally important to be clear that the Word of God is our *only guide* for a successful journey.

There have been and even now are those who take God's Word and twist it into what they want. Paul said to the Galatians, "I am amazed that you are so quickly deserting Him who called you by the grace of Christ, for a different gospel; which is really not another; only there are some who are disturbing you and want to distort the gospel of Christ" (Gal. 1:6-7 NASB).

As we journey on we will find that there will be some roadblocks, detours and ditches along the way. We should approach these situations with caution in our Christian journey. Before we continue into this next section, we need to be absolutely sure of who we are and whose we are. We need to be very sure about the message we believe and the message we are living. We need to be sure about our own conduct and character.

One of the hardest things to see is people so religiously committed to working for their eternal salvation only to find they will never have it. They have chosen the broad gate and the broad way. Jesus said of those kinds of people, "Not everyone who says to Me, 'Lord, Lord,' will enter the kingdom of heaven, but he who does the will of My Father who is in heaven will enter. Many will say to Me on that day, 'Lord, Lord, did we not prophesy in Your name, and in Your name cast out demons, and in Your name perform many miracles?' And then I will declare to them, 'I never knew you; Depart from Me, you who practice lawlessness'" (Matt. 7:21-23 NASB).

> "Check up on yourselves.
> Are you really Christians? Do you pass the test?
> Do you feel Christ's presence and power more and more within you?
> Or are you just pretending to be Christians when actually you aren't at all?"
> 2 Corinthians 13:5 (TLB)

# The Journey of Consequence

## Philippians 3

# 13

# The Journey Through Rejoicing
# Philippians 3:1

On a cool Saturday morning, Gayla and I drove to Globe, Arizona, about 100 miles north of Tucson. Our oldest daughter, Audra, who teaches high school there, isn't always able to visit with us during the school year. As I said before, I am not much for traveling, but the drive up there is rather enjoyable. The city of Globe is small, but it is a nice place to visit if you want to get away from it all.

At this time the steep, mountainous road between the town of Winkleman and Globe was being widened. Since they had to blast away part of the mountainside, the highway was closed on the weekdays. On the weekends, though, traffic still had to come to a monitored stop. Since the road was down to one lane, a lead car was there to take cars through the construction in each direction. We couldn't proceed until the lead car led us through. Sometimes the wait can be long. We were lucky. On the way up we waited for twenty minutes. On the way back we didn't have to wait at all. We had arrived just at the right time.

Like I said before, we could not proceed at this stop without the lead car. It was provided for our safety and the safety of others. Ignoring it would not only be dangerous, but foolish. In the first place, we had no way of knowing what was ahead, like the massive construction equipment coming at us or the oncoming traffic. In the second place, because it was only one lane, we had to be extremely careful, especially at night. The road under construction bordered the side of a cliff. If we got too close, we could be pushed into the canyon by falling debris.

Now to some it might seem annoying or like a waste of time, but to the State and to the road workers, it seemed like the best thing for everyone's safety. The lead car always proceeded with caution. It was on the lookout for the heavy equipment and could stop at a moment's notice if there was falling debris. We may not have liked it, but it was there for our own good.

I said all this because what follows in our journey is this command from Paul, "Finally, my brethren, rejoice in the Lord" (Philip. 3:1a NASB). The word *"finally"* anchors us to what has been said in the last two chapters and transitions into what is coming up ahead. Like the rearview mirror and windshield in our car, we can see where we have been and what is ahead.

Paul says, "Finally . . . rejoice." What does that mean? How are we to rejoice when our lives, our country and our world seem to be falling apart? Can God really do something in our world? Is there any hope of anything good coming out of what seems to be a very uncertain situation?

The answer to these questions is, "yes!" There is hope and there is good that can come out of all of this. I mentioned the lead car that took us from point A to point B. Without it we would have been in a very uncertain and dangerous situation. So here, the lead car in our journey is *"rejoicing."* Paul commands us to rejoice.

He also issues this command in other places in this letter. In chapters 2:18; 3:1 and 4:4 he commands the Philippians to *"rejoice."* He also tells the Thessalonians to *"rejoice always"* (1 Thess. 5:16 NASB). In the book of the Revelation it tells us that Christ has overcome and because of that we are commanded to *"rejoice."*

What does Paul mean when he says we need to *"rejoice?"* I find it amazing that Christians struggle with the essence of rejoicing. In fact, some Christians think that to rejoice or be in the state of rejoicing comes from external circumstances. If everything in our lives is going well then this joy, this rejoicing, will take place. But that can be totally misleading. What if everything isn't going well? What if, as a Christian, we have some illness or a financial crisis? What if there is a tragedy or some unforeseen circumstance that invades our lives? Would we still rejoice?

There are other Christians who feel that they have to emotionally psyche themselves up to be joyful. They think that by listening to

Christian music or preaching on the radio before church, they can somehow put themselves in a joyful mood. As ministers, don't we select music that is upbeat and rhythmic during the service in order to act on the emotions of the people worshiping there? I know, because I have done so. Sometimes, when I would plan the service, I would look for the music that excited and moved the worshiper.

In our world with so much uncertainty facing people today, is it any wonder that they turn to a variety of things? Is it any wonder that people turn to different things to bring them joy or happiness or some sense of fulfillment? Isn't that why people have turned to drugs or affairs or surround themselves in the fictitious? People are looking for something that can give them fulfillment in this chaotic life we live in.

But like every Christian, we frown upon such things. Our evangelistic approaches are designed to try and get people to see that depending on Jesus, on God Almighty, is the answer to their lack of fulfillment. We want them to face life realistically. We say and believe that only in Jesus can they have this fulfillment.

Listen, I am not living in some fantasy land. I know that most people have no desire for the things of God. The Bible tells us that the preaching of the Gospel is foolishness to worldly people and they have no time for it. This is why people we know, friends we work with, and our neighbors create this facade of happiness in their lives.

If we find this behavior wrong and unfulfilling in worldly people, then isn't it equally wrong for the believer? In a sense, it is false teaching to assume that we can cause some sort of joyfulness by targeting the emotions of other people or ourselves. It is also just as wrong to create a facade that we are always joyful. We plaster a smile on our faces, praise Jesus every moment we can, simply because we believe the world does not like a sour looking believer.

When Paul commands us to *"rejoice"* he is not telling us to force ourselves by playing to the emotions or pretending that everything is alright. Paul's circumstances dictate that he should really be miserable. Some are chiding him or attacking his teaching. But what does he do? He depends on Jesus. He surrenders his every heartbeat to the Gospel message. He rejoices because of whose he is.

If Paul were like most of us, had he been rejoicing in his own preaching or his own message, when the personal attacks came, he would be very hurt and discouraged. That is why I believe there are Christians who falter and fail—because they base their joy and fulfillment in their own abilities. When they are criticized or rebuffed, they resent it or just give up. But Paul's whole basis for rejoicing is in Jesus Christ and Him crucified. He says to the Galatians, "But may it never be that I would boast, except in the cross of our Lord Jesus Christ, through which the world has been crucified to me, and I to the world" (Gal. 6:14 NASB).

Paul was a realist. He knew life wasn't all some rainbow in the sky. He knew these Christians were going to face troubles that were outright unbearable but he commands them to *"rejoice."* Paul tells the Corinthians, "For while we are in this tent, we groan and are burdened . . . God . . . has given us the Spirit as a deposit . . . Therefore we are always confident . . . We live by faith, not by sight . . . So we make it our goal to please him, whether we are at home in the body or away from it" (2 Cor. 5:4-9 NIV).

So how then do we initiate this command to *"rejoice?"* Let me begin by first saying that in order to exercise this command we must first be sure of our relationship with Jesus Christ. We have to have the confidence that our position in Christ is perfect. The evidence of true rejoicing comes from having that assurance that God is working in us and that we are living a life that is pleasing to Him.

There is nothing in this world that will give the Christian confidence to rejoice. As we read about the current difficulties in our country right now, the news itself is very depressing. There seems to be this uneasiness in people and various tensions around our world. Our own personal lives are no better. Men and women find themselves looking for, searching for something that will give them certainty, comfort and even happiness in our world today.

So is it any wonder that people are medicating themselves with whatever will give them a sense of happiness? People are looking for something in this life that can give them a sense of fulfillment or happiness. The only people who really know anything about happiness are Christians. True rejoicing can only be experienced by the child of God.

We are called to be witnesses for Jesus, but sometimes I'm afraid that we send the wrong message. The Christian who is miserable, complaining or even unsure about himself and his current life situation is a bad testimony. This world is looking for the essence of true joy. So where will they find it if the only testimony we are giving is a negative one.

There is no greater time to let our light shine to a darkened world than today. If we are convinced that God has begun a good work in us, then our practice of that conviction should be evident. Jesus said, "Here on earth you will have many trials and sorrows. But take heart, because I have overcome the world" (John 16:33 NLT).

The Apostle Paul says, "And I am convinced that nothing can ever separate us from God's love. Neither death nor life, neither angels nor demons, neither our fears for today nor our worries about tomorrow—not even the powers of hell can separate us from God's love. No power in the sky above or in the earth below—indeed, nothing in all creation will ever be able to separate us from the love of God that is revealed in Christ Jesus our Lord" (Rom. 8:38-39 NLT).

As Christians, if what we say is true, if what we teach is true, if what we sing about is true, then it will be displayed in the way we live our lives. We are commanded to rejoice, to live our lives in that sphere of rejoicing, no matter what the circumstances are. We are called to show a life that goes against the feelings and ideas of what the world says is the answer to a miserable life. We are here to show that we can be more than conquerors.

So we are commanded to *"rejoice in the Lord."* But how is this done? Well, if we are to act on this command we must be willing to bring under control everything that brings us happiness or joy. In other words, if we are basing our joy or happiness on things that can easily be taken away or lost, then we are not experiencing true joy. We must refocus on this command and what it means to our lives.

We are on a journey and while we are here we must always remember to hold loosely the things that are temporal. If we find that our happiness is dependent upon certain things, then we need to correct it at once. We need to refocus. We must be careful about the foundations upon which we build our happiness. Paul said that, "No other foundation can a man lay than that which has been laid, which is Jesus Christ" (1 Cor. 3:11). So we must always be mindful of what is producing this happiness or this rejoicing.

Also, we must mediate on Jesus. If we are truly looking for this real sense of rejoicing then we must be willing to think about Him. Instead of letting ourselves be drawn away by the beauty and pleasure of other things, we must fix the eyes of our hearts on Jesus Christ. That is where true rejoicing must be centered and anchored to.

In the Wizard of Oz, the Scarecrow and Dorothy were traveling on the yellow brick road to see the Wizard. As they were traveling, their eyes were distracted by the apple trees off to the side. Instead of staying on the yellow brick road, they got off and went after the fruit that would give them pleasure and satisfaction. That decision got them into trouble. The trees came to life and started pitching apples at them.

We need to constantly focus our attention on Jesus. Paul says, "So we *fix* (contemplate) our eyes not on what is seen, but on what is unseen. For what is seen is temporary, but what is unseen is eternal" (2 Cor. 4:18 NIV). The writer of Hebrews says, "Let us *fix* (to look away from all else) our eyes on Jesus, the author and perfecter of our faith" (Heb. 12:2 NIV).

We should not only meditate on the person of Jesus, but also on His marvelous sacrifice. We should walk through His life from beginning to end. We should listen as He speaks to the crowds. Watch how He heals the hurting. We should weep as we see Him hanging on that cross. We need to think about what the cross means and why it was necessary for Him to endure this. We must see that it was for our sins that He left heaven's glory, became a servant, and was obedient unto death. We should rejoice at His resurrection. Finally, we should tell all about His coming once again.

We should meditate on these things and realize that this is not just another form of religious belief. It is not some philosophical idea. This is the plan of God. There is only one way to God and that is through Jesus Christ. We need to remember that He began a good work and that He is working it out in our lives to the very end.

Rejoicing can also be a safeguard for our spiritual lives. It can and should be the lead car that takes us through uncertainties, through never-ending strife and conflicts. The lead car keeps us from falling off the cliff of discouragement. Paul said, "Finally, my brethren, rejoice in the Lord. To write the same things again is no trouble to me, and it is a *safeguard* for you" (3:1 NASB). Like many parents, Paul says he doesn't mind repeating himself. What is at stake here is not loss of property or membership, but loss of spiritual fervency. He has used the word *rejoice* several times in this letter. That is what is at stake, the lack of rejoicing in the Christian life.

So it is not only important, but is also a safeguard. Here is why I see it as a safeguard. When we are rejoicing in the Lord, we will experience fewer difficulties in our journey through this life. The person who doesn't have a relationship with the Lord is already facing an upward climb in life. Life and its problems have more pressure on the unbeliever.

Is that to say that the person who is a believer is not going to have difficulties? No! What I am saying is that even though we encounter such things we have a foundation which we are anchored to which is Christ the Lord. Jesus said that the person who is anchored to the rock (rock bed of truth) will not suffer loss no matter what happens. But the person not anchored to the rock, but in the sand, will suffer loss (cf. Matthew 7:24-27).

Here is another reason I believe that rejoicing is a safeguard while on this journey to life. We will be faced with opposition from people who totally reject the Word of God. We have mentioned this earlier. There are many organizations that are seeking to and are implementing ways to destroy the Christian way of life and beliefs. We will also face perversion of the Word of God from other religious organizations. Listen, if we are committed to preaching the Word of God for His sake, then our rejoicing will keep us safe from our own egos. Remember, Paul has already told us not to do anything from conceit or vainglory.

Nehemiah said, "Do not be grieved, for the joy of the Lord is your strength" (Neh. 8:10 NASB). Rejoicing in the Lord gives us strength in times of loss and uncertainties. These Philippian Christians were deeply saddened because of Paul's situation. They also feared life without him. Yet, Paul tells them to rejoice in the Lord. Whether he would see them again or not, they were to keep their eyes on Christ.

You and I hold one of the greatest messages to a lost and dying world—the message of hope. People are looking for hope in something. They are looking for a hope that has a greater stability than the things of this life. What greater message could you and I give while we walk through this journey to joy, than to live a life of true rejoicing? One of the greatest reasons for rejoicing in the Lord is that Jesus will never fail us. His joy will never diminish. All of the happiness this world could ever give will ultimately fail.

Here is one of the greatest reasons we should rejoice in the Lord. You and I have been entrusted with something that even angelic beings can only look into. Here is the plan of God, salvation by grace through Jesus Christ. Here is the church, the body of Christ living out that plan and it has nothing to do with angels, but with frail human beings. What an honor we have been given. What a privilege we have been entrusted with. "His intent was that now, through the church, the manifold wisdom of God should be made known to the rulers and authorities in the heavenly realms" (Eph. 3:10 NIV).

> "So rejoice in him, all those who are his,
> and shout for joy,
> all those who try to obey him."
> (Psalms 32:11 TLB)

# 14

# The Journey Through Truth
# Philippians 3:2

Here in Arizona, you cannot beat the climate. It is usually great weather for anything your heart desires to do. If you like biking or hiking it is great weather. If you like outdoor sports like hunting and fishing, it is great weather. If you just like working in the yard or swimming in your pool it is really great weather. Even though it gets into the 100's during the summer, you cannot beat the weather here.

I am not saying there aren't any drawbacks to living here. We do have electrical storms and they can be very intense. We have strong winds and power outages at times. We also have the monsoon season here. These storms can dump a lot of rain in a hurry. Some of the local streets we have are used for water run offs. If you happen to be in these areas you have to be mindful of the strength these waters have as it dumps into these storm drains.

On occasion some of our underpasses have to be closed because of the water that collects in them. There are times when the water rises above the height of a normal car. On the top of these underpasses there is a sign that reads, *"Do not enter when flashing red light."* Now, even though these signs are clearly posted, some people will tempt fate. On numerous occasions some of these folks wind up on the ten o'clock news. Not something you would want a whole community to know.

Warning signs like these are not unusual. We see them on a variety of things. We see them on product labels. We see them posted on community pools or chain link fences that lead to military or industrial parks. We see them at construction sites and even in restaurants. They are there for your safety and for the safety of others.

On this journey to joy we see Paul's warning sign to the believers at Philippi. He says, "Beware of the dogs, beware of the evil workers, beware of the false circumcision" (Phil. 3:2 NASB). Three times he says, "Beware, beware, beware." Is this important? Yes! It is the flashing red light and we need to heed its caution.

What does he mean by this terminology; dogs, evil workers and the false circumcision? It's interesting that he uses terminology that the Judaizers were famous for using. The Judaizers were religious zealots who followed Paul everywhere he went and tried to undermine his message. Paul's demeanor here changes abruptly when he addresses these individuals. As you may recall, Paul makes mention of them in the previous two chapters. He says they were people looking to bring some sort of discouragement to him and his message. They were people who were out to destroy these young churches or to bring them in line with the predominant religion of that day which was Judaism. They also caused disunity and confusion in the young church.

So Paul wastes no time to call them to the forefront and expose them for who they were. Once again, the absence of true rejoicing in the believer's life leads to a life of arrogant and selfish agendas. Attending some denomination doesn't make you right, nor does it give you the right to demean another organization. To be a believer means you need to rise above the world's idea of right and wrong, truth and lies, and honesty as opposed to deception.

The first caution he gives these believers is "beware of the dogs." That is rather strange don't you think? Why would he compare these religionists to dogs? Well, in the first place, the Jewish people considered anyone not like them to be dogs. In Biblical times there were two groups, Jews and Gentiles. The Jews were the "chosen" and the Gentiles were not. This created friction between these two groups. One thought themselves (Jews) better than the other (Gentiles). If you would like to read further about these two groups go to *www.gty.org* and read Dr. John MacArthur's exposition on this subject.

So what does Paul mean when he says they were dogs? In the Greek, there are two words that describe this animal. One refers to a tamed dog. It would be considered a house pet. The other word describes a street dog. This is an animal that lives off the street with no guidance or discipline.

These animals rummage through the garbage of any back alley to feed off of. But they are also vicious and dangerous. One could say that living off the street for any length of time could cause any dog to go rabid.

I remember the first dog we had when I was a child. The dog was a black and white mixed breed. In all the years that we had him, though, he was always chained up. I remember being constantly warned by my mother not to get too close to him. He was a very angry dog and always seemed to salivate more than usual. I never liked playing in the backyard while he was there because I was afraid he would get loose and bite me. My fear of him made me fearful of other dogs as well. I recall one time our neighbor's Weiner dog (*yes, you read this right*) got loose and began to chase me. I ran for my life. I was so scared that I caught a fever because of it. The other kids laughed about it, but I didn't.

This is the image of the street dog that Paul is painting to these believers. He is saying that these people are undisciplined, scavengers and salivate over any opportunity to discredit God's message and His messenger. To Paul, the message of the Gospel, their joy and success were so critical that he is deliberately using this type of image. Nothing could be more devastating to the furtherance of the Gospel than people with the wrong view of the Gospel message.

It makes no difference to me what denominational name you call yourself. I have come to the belief that there are going to be a whole lot of denominational card carrying members on the wrong side of heaven. The thing about making the denominational name of great importance is that it leads to the same attitude as the scavenger dog. Today, we have some who will spend their time ripping apart other faiths by pointing out differences in traditional practices and foolish philosophies. Listen, the time has come, for us to stop pointing out the differences of religious practice and **start pointing to the One who can make a difference** in our lives and the lives of others. Pastor Rick Warren, of the Saddleback Church, is fond of saying it's not about me but, about Him, God.

In this journey to joy, truth has to be of great importance. Just like real rejoicing has nothing to do with playing to the emotions or the deliberate enforcement of being joyful, truth has to be first and foremost. We need to be truthful about ourselves concerning our character and conduct. If you've been involved in the church and church ministries you know how it can be at times. There are people who will simply act like dogs within the body. There is a constant barking and biting at one another over the silliest things.

This is why Paul tells these believers in the previous chapter that their character and conduct had to emulate that of Jesus Christ. He says they were to exemplify humility, selflessness, and unity (2:2). Street dogs do not care about other dogs. If another animal approaches their findings, they snarl and show their teeth and will do anything to protect their food. Street dogs also don't care how long food has been in the garbage or if it's even edible. They are in such a dysfunctional state that they cannot tell the difference between good food and rotten food.

As believers we can have a tendency to become dysfunctional in our Christian lives as well. That is why we are commanded to rejoice. One of the ways to protect ourselves from becoming undisciplined and dysfunctional is to base all our rejoicing on Him and Him alone. Our journey to joy can, at times, be hindered by our willingness to get off the path and feed on the things of this world. The world's idea of life is get all you can, can all you get and sit on the rest. That's a pretty good description of a street dog.

Paul was concerned about the impact this type of lifestyle would have on these young believers. Like a concerned parent he is warning them about these imposters, much like my mother warned me about our dog. In verses eighteen and nineteen of this chapter Paul reiterates his concern. "For many walk, of whom I often told you, and now tell you even weeping, that they are enemies of the cross of Christ, whose end is destruction, whose god is their appetite, and whose glory is in their shame, who set their minds on earthly things."

So beware, my friend, make sure that your Christianity is based on the Gospel, on God's Word, and not on the passing fancies of religious duties and philosophies. Remember to always measure yourself with the character of Christ. We will fall short at times, but God is always faithful to forgive us when we honestly admit we have run into a ditch.

Here is the next thing that Paul warns these believers about, "Beware of the evil workers." Wow! What is an evil worker? It is any person doing something that on the outside appears to be good or religious, but has, at its core, pride, vainglory or conceit. Listen, just because there are people doing good things, feeding the poor, going to church, or building houses for others is not an indication that they are a Christian. You can be the best person in the world, the most generous and most involved, but it is not a sign that you are a Christian.

We have been duped by this world into thinking that when we do good things, get involved in social or community services, somehow that makes us a Christian. We can do all the good works we want, but it still will lead us to a dead end. Jesus said of people like this, "Not everyone who says to Me, 'Lord, Lord,' will enter the kingdom of heaven, but he who does the will of My Father who is in heaven will enter. Many will say to Me on that day, 'Lord, Lord, did we not prophesy in Your name, and in Your name cast out demons, and in Your name perform many miracles?' And then I will declare to them, 'I never knew you; Depart from Me, you who practice lawlessness'" (Matt. 7:21-23 NASB).

Paul is saying that these religionists, the Judaizers, were doing things simply for pride's sake. They wanted the attention. It was all about them. Once again it goes against what Paul has previously told us that we are to do nothing out of selfish motives. The Jews could not work or earn their way to heaven. This was what Paul was saying to them. This is what Paul is saying to us as well. We can't work or earn our way to heaven either. Salvation is by grace and it is only by the grace of God that we enter into that relationship and receive that eternal reward.

In my ministry, I make it a practice not to accept anyone into church membership until I am sure of their salvation experience. Too many times in the churches where we have served, I've seen people come to church and be accepted without even verifying the fact that they have a personal relationship with Jesus Christ. It's a dangerous thing to give people a false sense of security just because they have joined YOUR church. It's equally dangerous to immediately put them to work in the church because it's their RELIGIOUS OBLIGATION. This does nothing but give people the sense that they have to do something in order to get to heaven.

Not much has changed from the time of Paul to today. We still have churches out there that teach and demand that you must go out and knock on doors and hand out materials in order to fulfill some religious mandate. Or light so many candles, walk so many miles or even pay homage to some religious figure. It isn't a question of living the free life in Jesus Christ, but of fulfilling a religious practice or satisfying some organizational precept.

So beware my friend, don't confuse activity for Christianity. The evidence of a redeemed life is one that manifests itself in character and conduct. Paul said that we are to have the same attitude about our lives that Jesus had, " . . . who, although He existed in the form of God, did not regard equality with God a thing to be grasped, but emptied Himself, taking the form of a bond-servant" (Phil. 2:6-7 NASB). We are called to serve not to be served. We serve a living and loving God. Paul encouraged the Philippians to " . . . join in following my example, and observe those who walk according to the pattern you have in us." (Phil. 3:17 NASB).

The final warning Paul gives us is "Beware of the false circumcision." Now, circumcision is something we have all heard of in some form or manner. But what does it mean here and why does Paul say these divisive characters were a false *circumcision*? Well, circumcision was established between God and Abraham as a sign of a covenant agreement between the two. In simple terms it was a sign that they were the chosen of God. These were the people God would move and speak through. You could say they were special.

The Greek word for circumcision that Paul uses here in his warning does not mean this covenant agreement. The word Paul uses describes physical mutilation. It was something that you do just to do it. It had no real value or purpose. In our world today many have undertaken the task of piercing themselves to appear different. The only problem with that is everyone else is doing it, also. So what started out to be a distinction, that you were not a part of the crowd, has become common.

It is the same idea here. What once was an action to define the Jew from the Gentile, or the chosen of God from everyone else, was now something that was made common. Circumcision, the actual cutting of the foreskin for class distinction, had no real relevance in the Christian church. This action no longer made that distinction and in Paul's view it was just an act of mutilation. What he is saying is that external actions are not enough to prove you are of God.

People who say, "Well they are doing the best they can, they are trying," just don't understand what it is to be a Christian or what makes a Christian. Closeness only counts in horseshoes and hand grenades. And in this journey to joy we must know, we must have that conviction, that confidence that God is working in our lives. Here is the problem with churches that pass out a feel good, come as you are message. They are misleading people and are preaching a false Gospel. Being good and doing good works and belonging to some denominational organization is no indication that you are a Christian.

The Jews wanted to add something to the message of grace. They wanted these new believers to continue in the old ways. They felt that just because they had this external distinction they were the true believers and everyone else had to fall in line with them and their teaching. Paul says in his letter to the Romans, "For he is not a Jew who is one outwardly, nor is circumcision that which is outward in the flesh. But he is a Jew who is one inwardly; and circumcision is that which is of the heart, by the Spirit, not by the letter; and his praise is not from men, but from God" (Rom. 2:28-29 NASB).

Now you may be a member of a local denomination or a non-denominational church and you may be faithful in your going and giving and doings, but if you have never asked Jesus into your heart, you are as lost as lost can be. We have done a major disservice to people who come and join our fellowship when we fail to show them that it is Jesus and only Jesus that can give them grace. If you are counting on your church membership to get you into heaven, quit now and enjoy the rest of your life. Without Jesus there is no hope.

Gayla and I have visited many different churches in these last few months. I must say with a deep sense of concern that there is very little substance in the messages given. I have come to the conclusion that the reason our world has slipped so far into chaos is because the message of the ages has gotten lost in the building of our own little kingdoms. We have and cherish our own circumcision. You can call it denomination, you can call it serving or you can even call it giving. But what you can't call it is Christianity.

Before we enter into the next section, let's stop for a moment and focus on the warning light that may have come on while you were reading this. Is the life you are now living the life that pleases God? That's an honest question to ask. It doesn't matter what I think or what other people think. It should matter to you what God thinks. Nobody is perfect and Christians especially should know they are not perfect. But what you need is to really stop and ask, "Is God really working in my life?" He is committed to finishing the work, but is there this conviction, this stirring in your heart that He has actually started the construction?

Like many believers I look back at my life and shake my head at all the dumb, costly choices I have made. There is no way to get back those years. I am on this journey just like you and I struggle at times to keep going. It isn't easy and the Bible makes it very clear that it will not be easy. But we are called to fight through it and depend on the power that is available to get us through to the end.

So, is there a warning light flashing in your life right now? If there is, stop for a moment and heed the caution. The Bible promises us that there is no temptation we will ever face that the power of God cannot overcome (1 Cor.10:13).

> "Those who listen to instruction will prosper;
> those who trust the Lord will be joyful."
> Proverbs 16:20 (NLT)

# 15

# The Journey Through True Christianity pt. 1
# Philippians 3:3

I am probably dating myself here, but do you remember the show, "To Tell the Truth?" Here were three individuals that all claimed to be this one person. One would say "I am Clyde Poindexter." Then another one would say, "NO, I am Clyde Poindexter." And then the third one would say, "No, I AM Clyde Poindexter." Then a panel would have to seek out the real Clyde Poindexter. They would ask a series of questions to find out the truth. After all of the information had been gathered, they would prove who the real Clyde Poindexter was.

That is what I believe our world is doing today. They are looking for and asking questions about who the real Christians are. There are so many organizations claiming to be Christian that it is impossible to tell which is the real thing. They all seem to be doing good things, saying the right things or living in a right way. But does that constitute a Christian? John in his first epistle tells us, "These things I have written to you . . . so that you may know" (1 John 5:13 NASB). But know what? The problem with a lot of Christians is that they do not know whether they are a Christian or not. If Christians are not sure about who they are, then how is a lost world going to know who Jesus is?

As Christians can we really know who we are with great assurance? The answer is, "Yes!" We have no excuse for not knowing. I mentioned earlier that the Christian life comes with its own GPS, God's Powerful Spirit. The Word of God is also a guiding tool for a successful walk or, in this case, a successful journey to joy. Listen, these letters were written so that we would have a certainty in life. Christians who live a teeter-totter kind of life have a misconception of how important the Word of God is in their lives.

In 1John 5:13-21, John tells us we can have this assurance, this knowledge. Now what assurances can we have? He says we can be assured of *eternal life*. When we place our trust in Him to save us and lead us, we have assurance that we can have life with Him now and in the hereafter. We don't have to wonder and worry about what is out there. We don't have to be like James T. Kirk from "Star Trek" wondering about what lies beyond the stars.

Also, when we enter into a relationship with God, we have, "*Confidence* . . . that, if we ask anything according to His will, He hears us" (v.14). He is a personal God who is living and active in our lives. It seems to me that so many Christians walk around as if God has passed away. We're like the disciples, when they heard that Jesus had died they just went out to restart their lives. God is very much alive and we should know it and can know it and there is no excuse for not knowing it because, "we know that He hears us in whatever we ask, we know that we have the requests which we have asked from Him" (v.15). A dead deity cannot hear or respond, but a God that is ever living, never dying, always loving, will listen and will respond. That is an active relationship and we cannot get that from a tree or an ideal or some philosophy or denominational identity.

We can also have assurance that we are in a relationship with God when what breaks God's heart breaks ours. John goes on to say, "If anyone sees his brother committing a sin not leading to death, he shall ask and God will for him give life to those who commit sin not leading to death" (v.16). If we are demonstrating compassion, then there will be no room for selfish vengeance. "There is a sin leading to death; I do not say that he should make request for this" (v.16).

Believers *know* and *recognize* the sin in their lives and the potential to give in to sin in their lives. John says, "All unrighteousness is sin, and there is a sin not leading to death. We know that no one who is born of God sins; but He who was born of God keeps him, and the evil one does not touch him" (vs.18).

Believers know that this world is *controlled and dominated* by the devil. There is an unseen battle that, we, as believers, should be aware of. "We know that we are of God, and that the whole world lies in the power of the evil one" (v.19)

Believers have this *certainty* about them, that Jesus is real and that He is the only way. He is not one of the ways; He is THE ONLY WAY. I marvel at the way our country is bending backwards to compensate for other religious organizations. While I believe in the freedom of speech and the freedom to worship in any way you like, I am not willing to concede nor should the Christian community concede that there are other ways to eternal life.

During my time serving one of the local churches here, I was really dismayed that some of the churches in this association were partnering with worldly organizations who blatantly denied the deity and lordship of Jesus Christ. When I wrote to state my displeasure over it, I was labeled as an intolerant bigot who was full of himself. But the very founder of this denomination was a committed believer in the Word of God. He stood on its principles and power.

Here's the thing, you cannot be a Christian or call yourself a Christian organization if you deny the lordship and deity of Jesus. John says, "And we know that the Son of God has come, and has given us understanding so that we may know Him who is true; and we are in Him who is true, in His Son Jesus Christ. This is the true God and eternal life" (v.20). The popular thing today is to give credibility to those religious organizations simply because they have shown tremendous growth in our country and around the world. So I am sure that I will not be popular when I say that Jesus and ONLY JESUS is the way to eternal life.

Finally, John says "Little children, guard yourselves from idols" (v.21). We all have our own little idols. You can call it what you want, sports, money, food, cars, entertainers or whatever, we all have them. An idol is anything that draws your attention, and you think of first and foremost. Even religious denominations or religious figures have become idols to many of us. John warns believers to guard ourselves from the things that so easily entice us. The Apostle Peter tells us, "You therefore, beloved, knowing this beforehand, be on your guard so that you are not carried away by the error of unprincipled men and fall from your own steadfastness" (2 Pet. 3:17 NASB).

So we come now to the understanding of what a Christian is. Paul has warned us of those that give the illusion of Christianity, but are not. Jesus said of people like this, "Beware of the false prophets, who come to you in sheep's clothing, but inwardly are ravenous wolves" (Matt. 7:15 NASB). I like the way the Message Bible states this same verse, "Be wary of false preachers who smile a lot, dripping with practiced sincerity.

Chances are they are out to rip you off some way or other. Don't be impressed with charisma; look for character."

This is why Paul emphatically says three times to "beware" of people who give the pretense of Christianity, but are not Christians (3:2). You and I need to be equally sure of the life we proclaim to be living. Just because we may be charismatic does not mean we are truly born again. Jesus warns us that character, not charisma, is important. There has been so much collateral damage done by charismatic people disguised as a Christian. Jesus said the way to know for sure about someone is by the fruit they bear.

True Christianity is this, "for we are the true circumcision, who worship in the Spirit of God and glory in Christ Jesus and put no confidence in the flesh." (Phil. 3:3 NASB). Now, I want to take my time in defining the Christian life because I am mindful that many good and decent people have a misconception of what a Christian is. I am also fearful, that many who read this book may think that just taking an idea or two and applying it to their lives will demonstrate that they are a Christian or make them a better Christian.

The purpose for writing this book was not so that you could take this idea or that idea to make you a better person or to give you some false sense of being a Christian. Everything I have written about thus far is all about the Christian life in its entirety. I want us to be clear on that. I cannot stress enough to you how important it is to be absolutely sure about the Christian life. Countless people have ended up in the ditches of life simply because they had a wrong view or have been misled concerning the Christian life. So, it is with a very concerned pastoral heart that I want to spend some time in this part of our journey.

In his letters, Paul seems to always give a description of what a Christian is. He does this because there were many in the Jewish sect that tried to prevent the message of grace from superseding obedience to Jewish ordinances. They wanted to hold on to the old ways. He also did it because there was a tendency in the new church to forget this marvelous message of grace. So he gives these definitions of a Christian and how a Christian is to live. In other words, he says the fruit of the Christian life is this.

Here again he says, "For we are the true circumcision." We said before that circumcision was an outward sign of being set aside for the purposes of God. The Jews felt that because they had been circumcised they were the only true people of God. But Paul refutes that and says that the true people of God are those who have been circumcised inwardly. It was a spiritual experience not a surgical procedure.

So, true Christianity is not just some outward activity. The Jews were determined to hold on to this external evidence and we are not much different today. Some people in churches claim to be Christian because of the some of the things they do. So I want to set the stage for what a true Christian is by stating what Christianity is not. The first thing we need to realize is that to be a Christian is not something that is external.

In the movie "Leap Of Faith" Steve Martin plays a traveling evangelist. On the outside he seems to be this genuine, powerful preacher, but as the movie progresses we find that he is a shyster, a con artist. We need to make sure that we are not just clothing our lives with a pretense of Christianity.

Now you may be a fine upstanding moral person, but that does not make you a Christian. There are a lot of fine and decent people who have no time for God nor care much about Him. But still, they are kind and decent people. Also, just because you have a basic belief that God exists or that Jesus is His Son, or that some of the stories in the Bible are true does not make you a Christian. Our world is constantly trying to define the Christian life by external actions. So we need to heed the words that Peter spoke, "be on your guard so that you are not carried away by the error of unprincipled men and fall from your own steadfastness" (2 Pet. 3:17 NASB).

Neither does following certain religious guidelines, practices or disciplines make you a Christian. So much has been made of traditional practices and dietary regimen that the wonder and splendor of the message of grace has been lost. Finally, just because you attend a worship service, sing songs of praise or attend a Bible study, does not make you a Christian.

All of these things we have mentioned are a **part** of the Christian life, but they are not the thing that makes us Christians. You and I cannot live the Christian life simply by doing certain things or not doing certain things. That is why Paul says at the beginning of this chapter that he has no trouble repeating himself. That is why he constantly gives us these short, definitive examples of what a Christian is and does.

Too many decent people have gone into eternal darkness because leaders in the church have confused grace with activity. Look around you. In our world today preachers stand on large stages and claim that if you give generously to their ministries you will receive a blessing from God. These people never mention that, only a child of God can truly receive His blessing. The Gospel message has nothing to say to the unbeliever except that he is lost and needs the grace of God.

Other preachers say all you need to have is faith in God, but they never mention that we need to ask Jesus into our hearts in order to be a true member of His family. Also, we have preachers who devise systems of belief that encourages people to live any way they want. They teach, "If it feels good, do it", but people like this are not true believers. They are true deceivers. These are the very people Jesus warns us about. These people are nothing more than wolves in sheep's clothing.

As I watch some of these televangelists, I am horrified at some of the erroneous doctrines they propagate. I am amazed at how they pervert and misquote the Word of God. I cannot even contain myself when they parade people on some stage and by some unseen power, force the Spirit of Jesus on them.

Jesus is not some vitamin we take daily. The Gospel is not the GOS-PILL as some well-meaning Christians like to state it. The Gospel message is the Living Word. He is the only One that can give us life and light throughout our journey to joy. For people to claim anything short of this is heresy and will be damned by the Lord Jesus Christ. How haunting are these word of Jesus Christ, "And then I will declare to them, 'I never knew you; Depart from Me, you who practice lawlessness'" (Matt. 7:23 NASB).

I am reminded of the song that has these words in it, "Change my heart O God, make it ever true, change my heart O God may I be like You" (CCLI Song # 1565 Written By: Eddie Espinosa Copyright: © 1982 Mercy/Vineyard Publishing ). Only Jesus can satisfy our soul. Only Jesus can make us whole. And only Jesus will lead us home. Is this not what our heart's should desire?

# 16

# The Journey Through True Christianity pt. 2
# Philippians 3:3-11

I am a Beatles' fan. I remember the day they hit the streets of America. Every girl and boy in our school started to dress like them and sing their songs rather loudly during lunchtime. I always wanted to play the guitar like them and have the same clothes they wore. In my day they were cool, (We used another word for cool but I don't think it would be appropriate to use it here). These four young men from England took this country by storm.

Not too long ago a friend of mine invited me to a Beatles' concert at one of the local casinos. Of course, this group was nothing more than impersonators. What I found so amazing was that when they played, it was as if we were actually seeing the real thing. They had images of the real Beatles flashing up on huge screens and every so often they would pan down to the guys on the stage. From the guitars, to the clothes and even to the vocals, if I hadn't known better, I would have sworn that they were the real Beatles. I had all these goose bumps running up and down my arms. I have seen other young men perform the same music with all the clothes and guitars, but none of them were as real as these guys.

They gave such an indisputable representation of the real thing that from a distance we couldn't tell that they weren't. But when the cameras zoomed in on them, we could see all the flaws and differences from the real Beatles. So, I wonder, if it is possible for young men like these to give such a representation of the real thing, is it possible that we could also give such a representation of the Gospel message? Could some who call themselves Christians represent the image of God so closely and yet not be the real thing?

From a distance it is possible to look like, sound like and even give the impression that we are Christians. But I want us to use the zoom lens of the Word of God to discover the truth about ourselves and the truth about real Christianity. Paul says that we are the true circumcision "who worship in the Spirit of God" (3:3). Here we come to this first understanding of what a true Christian is. A true Christian is someone who has had an internal transformation. They are people who not only have the externals right, but have had an internal renewal. Something inside the heart of that person has changed.

The Jews prided themselves on external evidences. They had the Law and the ceremonies and the practice of circumcision down. These were the things that they held up high as the sign that they were the people of God. We are no different today. We brag about how spiritual we are because we go to this church or we go to church three times a week or we do other things at the church. But Paul says that is not what makes you and me a Christian.

He says that true Christians are people who have had a change of heart. They are people who worship God in the Spirit or *who worship by the Spirit of God*. So what is worship and what does it mean to worship by the Spirit of God? Well, I am sure you are well aware that in the church today there are all kinds of ways to worship. There are different bodies claiming to have the one true way or a better and more spiritual way to worship. The modern church says worship is having this type of music or this type of preaching. They are well-tapped into the 21$^{st}$ century of modernism.

Other groups say, "No, to really worship there has to be this type of building, this way of doing music and preaching in this manner in order to claim to have been to worship." Here again, we have a tendency to define worship by the externals. As Paul refutes the claims of the religionists of his day, he also refutes what we are claiming as true worship in our churches in the 21$^{st}$ century.

"True worship," he says "comes by the Spirit of God." This can only happen when the Spirit of God resides in our hearts. True worship is personal not external. True worship begins in the heart of the believer not in the building or the method. Is it any wonder that the church today is anemic? Is it any wonder that you find yourself battling to go to church or even having the desire to go to church? I know how you feel. I find myself from time to time struggling to go to any church. Why? Because, like many of you, I have sometimes made worship mechanical and not personal.

So how do we break from the mechanical type of worship to the personal experience of worship? Once again let me restate this, you must have a personal relationship with Jesus. That is the beginning, the foundation upon which we build. Without this we are just building on sand.

The next thing that we need to really consider is how we worship. Consider this, in your quiet time, do you require some form of music and message to commune with God? By this I mean, do you feel you have had an intimate experience with God because you heard Christian music or listened to someone preaching to get you into that experience? Or was it simply that you came humbly before the Lord and communed with Him? So why is it that we depend on these things in the local church in order to claim that we have been in worship?

The Jews were unwilling to give up the external evidences. This is why they fought with Paul and invaded the Christian churches. They felt that form not conversion was the only way to be a true follower of God. The 21st century church that makes that same demand is no different than these worldly religionists.

True worship is by the Spirit; the believer is prompted by the Spirit and moved by the Spirit. To be a true Christian is to realize that the externals are not what make us a Christian. Jesus said to the woman at the well, "Believe me, dear woman, the time is coming when it will no longer matter whether you worship the Father on this mountain or in Jerusalem . . . the time is coming . . . when true worshipers will worship the Father in spirit and in truth . . . For God is Spirit, so those who worship him must worship in spirit and in truth" (John 4:21-24 NLT).

True worship is also not a matter of duty or requirement, but of knowing and being moved by the Spirit of God. In other words, we don't go to church because we have to. We don't go as a matter of responsibility or to fulfill our commitment to the church rules and guidelines. Many of us, as we were growing up, were forced to go to church. We didn't like it, but we went at the urging of our parents. Even now, we may have carried that mentality over to our adult life and feel that we have to go as a matter of responsibility. That is not worship. True worship is knowing that something inside of us is moving us, stirring our heart and we have a deep desire to go.

True worship is always loving and intimate. It is never cold and indifferent. When we worship by the Spirit, we show our love and gratitude for God the Father. We love Him and show our love for Him because of who He is and what He has done. Along with that, when we truly worship by the Spirit, we come to realize the very presence of God. We may have a tendency to think of God as some ominous force somewhere out there in the cosmos. When we put ourselves in submission, we have the Force around us. But God is not a force but a personal being. He is our God and Father. He is loving and gracious. He is merciful and forgiving. He is active and present daily.

True worship is coming to the realization and being convinced that God is truly working in our lives. We sense it. We see it as our lives are changing daily. Nothing could be more powerful in the life of the believer than to know we are in a relationship with this Almighty God who deserves our admiration and respect. Even greater still is knowing that in our relationship with God Almighty, He is a father, a loving parent with whom we can be intimate. No form, practice or location can ever give us that intimacy.

Here is a second description of a true believer. A true believer not only worships God in the Spirit, but also "glories in Christ Jesus." The word *"glory"* in the Greek is actually the word *"boast."* It means to shout out loudly or to basically brag about Jesus Christ. I attend a pastors' breakfast from time to time and occasionally someone comes in and starts blowing his horn about his accomplishments or activities. He's like one of those horns they have at football games. When the home team makes a touchdown they blow off this horn. Everyone can hear it and it is loud.

The Jews were bragging about their accomplishments and the external evidence they had of being the chosen. Once again Paul says that to be truly the chosen of God we have to be willing not to brag about ourselves, but about Jesus Christ. To be a true Christian means to be proud of Jesus. Have you ever been embarrassed to tell people about yourself, or your family or where you work or even where you go to church? Paul says, the true evidence of whether or not a person is a Christian is this, are they bragging about Jesus or themselves?

You see, the test of true Christianity comes when we realize all the things Christ has done for us. The fact that He came to us, became a servant for us and gave His life for us should cause us to brag about Jesus. Paul tells us all of this in Philippians chapter two. Jesus exposes the sin in our lives, the very thing that keeps us from a relationship with God. He has paid that price so that we could have an intimate relationship with the Father. Without the cross of Christ we would have no way to get to heaven.

Paul says he doesn't mind bragging about the cross of Christ. He says, "May I never boast except in the cross of our Lord Jesus Christ, through which the world has been crucified to me, and I to the world. Neither circumcision nor uncircumcision means anything; what counts is a new creation" (Gal. 6:14-15 NIV). So if you find yourself bragging about your own accomplishments more than about Jesus and what He has done, then maybe you need to stop and examine yourself.

Then finally he says this, "For we are the true circumcision, who worship in the Spirit of God and glory in Christ Jesus and *put no confidence in the flesh*" (3:3). Here the word for *"confidence"* in the Greek means to *"persuade."* It carries the idea of trying to convince ourselves that by doing certain things or following certain things we are Christians.

That is what the Jews were doing. They were trying to persuade these young churches that all of the external things they did constituted the Christian life. That is one of the traps we have a tendency to fall into. We have this idea that if we do certain things, give a certain amount, attend so many services and Bible studies then we are spiritual. We try and convince ourselves that all these external activities will make us Christians. This is what Paul means by, "put no confidence in the flesh." What makes him a Christian is not activity but an intimate relationship with Jesus. He knows God is working in his life. He is convinced of that.

Paul goes on to say that we cannot even enter into heaven by joining some religious organization. He says that if this was possible, then he would be right at the front of the line. He tells us, that as a Jew, his bloodline or his heritage was of great significance. He says to these religionists, "If you want to make your case based on these things then so can I." "If anyone else has a mind to put confidence in the flesh, I far more: circumcised the eighth day, of the nation of Israel, of the tribe of Benjamin, a Hebrew of Hebrews" (Phil. 3:4-5 NASB).

You could have been born in a Christian family, to parents who are missionaries or been the child of a pastor, but that does not qualify you to be a Christian. There are people who believe that. They feel that just because mom and dad were Christians and they belonged to a church then that makes them a Christian, also. That makes about as much sense as saying that just because I drink a lot of tomato juice, one day I will become a tomato.

Then Paul goes on to say that if my heritage does not make me a Christian neither can my achievement. Again he places himself at the top of the list. "As to the Law, a Pharisee; as to zeal, a persecutor of the church; as to the righteousness which is in the Law, found blameless" (Phil. 3:5-6 NASB). He is saying that he had aspired to be the best of the best. He had accomplished his goals and was in every way, shape and form the most dedicated to the cause. Once again he exposes the foolishness of these religionists by saying that none of these things were important to him now that he had met Jesus. He was now a new creation, a devoted follower of God and a proud proclaimer of Jesus Christ. He was willing to count everything as worthless for the sake of knowing Jesus and growing in Him.

Paul goes on to say, "But whatever things were gain to me, those things I have counted as loss for the sake of Christ. More than that, I count all things to be loss in view of the surpassing value of knowing Christ Jesus my Lord, for whom I have suffered the loss of all things, and count them but rubbish so that I may gain Christ, and may be found in Him, not having a righteousness of my own derived from the Law, but that which is through faith in Christ, the righteousness which comes from God on the basis of faith, that I may know Him and the power of His resurrection and the fellowship of His sufferings, being conformed to His death; in order that I may attain to the resurrection from the dead" (Phil. 3:7-11 NASB).

Here he is saying that he was willing to suffer the loss of all the things that the Jews held on to so dearly for the sake of growing in Christ. He was well aware that his efforts in the Law and the practice of it would not give him the right to enter into the kingdom of heaven. He sees that submitting in faith to Christ will be counted as righteousness by God. He understands that this relationship would give him the power to endure the hardship he was facing. He also is convinced that what he would lose in earthly terms would certainly be gained in eternal reward.

What is more important to you reputation or relationship? What do you point to so that people will know you are a child of God—your self-effort or your undying devotion to Jesus? When you sacrifice your time or money or material things, what brings you more pleasure, the praise of men or the knowledge that you are serving God Himself?

> "Now, little children, abide in Him,
> so that when He appears,
> we may have confidence and not shrink away
> from Him in shame at His coming.
> If you know that He is righteous,
> you know that everyone also
> who practices righteousness is born of Him."
> 1 John 2:28-29 (NASB)

# 17

# The Journey Through Living The Christian Life
# Philippians 3:12-16

I read the other day about a woman who was struck by lightning and was in a coma for several days. As the family gathered around her, the doctors were careful not to give false hope. Within a matter of days she came out of the coma. Even though she has spent time in rehab, she is happy to be interacting with her family. I also know of others who have been struck by lightning or for some other reason have slipped into a coma never again to relate to those around them. They have all the necessary medical equipment to make them look like they are living, but in reality, they are not. It doesn't make them less human, but the coma prevents them from relating to those around them.

In the Christian life, just because we may have the essentials of the Christian life right, is no indication that we are truly living the Christian life. I tried to demonstrate, what it means to be a Christian, in the previous two chapters. There are certain things that lead us to know that we are truly in an intimate relationship with God the Father. To put it another way, we can know for certain that God has begun a good work in us based on what we have already discussed.

Having just the essentials down and not living them out is where many of us end up in a ditch. So Paul says to us here that not only do we need to have the essentials right, but we need to live them out. There has to be evidence or fruit that is displayed in our lives. Paul tells Timothy to beware of people who have the appearance of godliness, but who are deceived and are trying to deceive others. He says that these people are, " . . . holding to a form of godliness, although they have denied its power; Avoid such men as these" (2 Tim. 3:5 NASB).

Paul, therefore, uses his life's testimony to disprove what these religious imposters were saying was true Christianity. As we look at his testimony it is something that you and I need to reflect on daily. Why? Because the Christian life is a daily walk. Many of us are quite comfortable to walk the Christian walk on Sundays and Wednesdays, but living the Christian life is a daily interaction with God. We can hook ourselves up to a Bible study, a church worship, the praise team or to the pulpit. Yet, if the only thing that these external activities do is just keep us on life support, or better yet, keep the image of us living the Christian life, then we are no better than the people Paul warned Timothy about.

The Apostle Paul says this, "Not that I have already obtained it or have already become perfect, but I press on so that I may lay hold of that for which also I was laid hold of by Christ Jesus." (Phil. 3:12 NASB). What is he saying? Well, he is saying that the person who has truly entered into an intimate relationship with God through Jesus Christ knows that there is something greater controlling their life. He says, "But I press on so that I may lay hold of that for which also I was laid hold of by Christ Jesus" (v.14). It is the same idea he has stated in chapter one, verse six, where he says, "for I am confident of this very thing, that *He who began a good work in you* will perfect it until the day of Christ Jesus."

The Christian life is a life of knowing that something greater has influenced our lives. We know that our daily life is being guided or controlled by that spiritual presence or, better yet, Person. Something or someone has grabbed us, captured us or, to take it a step further, enslaved us. We are under this mighty power, this influence. That is what Paul is saying, God has captured him, seized him and he not only knows this, but welcomes it. That is why he was so confident about the things he willingly gave up. They brought him no pleasure, no hope and all of his self-effort was of no profit to him.

So true Christian living is not only knowing and realizing that God has taken hold of our lives, but that we have not yet arrived. In other words, when we gave our hearts and lives to Jesus, we were not automatically perfect. We have the propensity to sin. Does that ever go away? No, the influence of this world, the attraction of the things around us sometimes causes us to get off the journey. That is why Paul says this, "Not that I have already obtained it or have already become perfect" (v.12).

That is part of the problem with people and more specifically denominational teachings that say that we are already made perfect. They teach we became sinless the moment we gave our hearts to Jesus. Paul says that is not true, however. He tells us that even he did not have this perfection. The religionists of his day felt that they were already perfect because of their heritage and achievements. Once again Paul says this is false. He says that true Christian living comes from admitting that self-effort leads to a dead end. True Christian living comes from acknowledging that true righteousness comes from God through faith in Jesus Christ.

Dr. MacArthur once said, "My position in Christ is perfect. It is matching my practice with my position." That is what Paul means when he says, "Not that I have already obtained it or have already become perfect." He tells us earlier in this letter to, "work out your salvation." He says that we need to be "of the same mind, maintaining the same love, united in spirit, intent on one purpose" (2:2 NASB). He goes on to say that we need to regard others as more important, not to be vain or conceited, but humble. All of these things are flaws in our lives that will take time to correct. It is only through the power of Christ that it can be accomplished. That is what I believe Dr. MacArthur meant when he said, "It is matching my practice with my position."

True Christian living is also recognizing the battle within us, the battle to fulfill foolish desires as opposed to fulfilling the purposes of God in our lives. Paul says, "but I press on so that I may lay hold of that" (v.12). The phrase "press on" carries the idea of "pursuing after." This is probably best illustrated by a runner in a race. If you've ever seen the Olympics you've seen these guys running, always keeping their eyes on what is ahead. They have to have an unwavering determination. There are a lot of things around them that can cause them to look away from their goal. There are people cheering and cameras flashing. If one of these runners loses his focus, he could stumble and not reach the finish line. That is what Paul has in mind here.

As one of the most visible characters in the New Testament, Paul recognized that focus was most important. In order to keep on this journey, Paul had to continually battle his desire to do that which pleased him as opposed to that which pleased God. Paul said, "I have discovered this principle of life—that when I want to do what is right, I inevitably do what is wrong. I love God's law with all my heart. But there is another power within me that is at war with my mind. This power makes me a slave to the sin that is still within me" (Rom. 7:21-23 NLT). We all have this struggle. To say otherwise is to not be truthful.

True Christian living is not being content to reach a certain level of spiritual maturity. Paul says, "Brethren, I do not regard myself as having laid hold of it yet; but one thing I do: forgetting what lies behind and reaching forward to what lies ahead" (Phil. 3:13 NASB). We should never be satisfied with where we're at in our spiritual walk. Just because we do not live the same kind of life as before does not mean we have reached that stage of perfection.

We should also be extremely careful not to pride ourselves in being better than others. We are a work in progress. In order to come to this place there has to be self-examination. Paul says he had not yet reached that life of perfection. He could not say that unless he had not evaluated his life against the life of Jesus. He understood the standard was not religious conformity and self-effort, but one of complete surrender.

True Christian living is not *relying on past spiritual experiences*. Paul says, "but one thing I do: forgetting what lies behind" (v.13). There is this tendency to look back at past accomplishments as if to draw some equity off those experiences. It's like the runner in the race looking back to see how far he has come or to see how far he is from all other runners. Paul is saying that the person looking back at past accomplishments to measure their spirituality is in danger of losing the race or better still not finishing this journey.

True Christian living is *keeping our focus on the ultimate goal of God*. Paul says, "reaching forward to what lies ahead." In the Greek, the word *"reaching"* has the imagery of a runner stretching forward to grab the ribbon at the finish line. There are a lot of reasons why we might not finish the race. However, the fact is that the Christian life is not passive but one of determination. Paul previously told us to, "work your our salvation with fear and trembling; for it is God who is at work in you, both to will and to work for His good pleasure" (2:12-13 NASB). There is our part and then there is God's part.

What is at the end of this race that Paul so adamantly says he is reaching for? What is this prize that we are to focus on? Well, to put it simply, it is the ultimate goal of perfection in Christ and the complete assurance of eternal living with Him. Remember in verse six of chapter one of Philippians Paul said that he was confident of God working in his life? Well, he was also confident that if he remained faithful in his walk with Jesus, continued to grow and learn daily, that God would complete him. In other words, he would become what God's ultimate purpose was for him.

Paul says in the last few verses, "For our citizenship is in heaven, from which also we eagerly wait for a Savior, the Lord Jesus Christ; who will transform the body of our humble state into conformity with the body of His glory, by the exertion of the power that He has even to subject all things to Himself" (Phil. 3:20-21 NASB). John says in his Epistle, "Beloved, now we are children of God, and it has not appeared as yet what we will be. We know that when He appears, we will be like Him, because we will see Him just as He is" (1 John 3:2 NASB).

The ultimate goal is to be like Him, not only when we get there, but to have the same attitude that Paul had from the very beginning of his conversion. This is the daily goal of true Christian living. The lives and convictions of the Apostles recorded in the New Testament are not just for bedtime reading. They are the pattern, a template for living the Christian life. Paul says once again, "Brethren, join in following my example, and observe those who walk according to the pattern you have in us" (Phil. 3:17 NASB).

Paul is speaking here to those who are spiritually mature, those who have moved on from milk to meat, "Let us therefore, as many as are perfect, have this attitude; and if in anything you have a different attitude, God will reveal that also to you" (v.15). He is not saying that some had attained perfection. We have already seen that is not what Paul believed. He does mean that there has to be a progressive growth in our spiritual walk. We cannot remain infants in the Christian life. We must also come to understand that in the essentials there can be no compromise, but in the nonessentials, each one must be guided by what God leads that individual to do.

Finally, true Christian living is never *wavering from the truth of the Gospel*. Paul says, "Let us keep living by that same standard to which we have attained" (v.16). He is saying that there can be no compromise in the way we approach the Christian life. There is no other way to achieve growth as a Christian. We cannot do it by self-effort or by joining denominational organizations. True Christian living comes by having a relationship with Jesus and learning and growing in Him.

Paul exemplified the standard of true Christian living to these believers. The Judaizers put up their external facts of what a true follower of God was to be like. Today, there are some religious groups that teach that you have to do something in order to be saved or in order to be assured of your salvation. They point to their external evidences and say that is what true followers of God do.

Paul says, "No." True followers are those who have their heart changed and are being changed from one level of glory to another level of glory. Paul says that we must become a new creation. Peter says we must have a desire for the Word of God. John tells us that we must come to the place where we know that we are Christians. James tells us that we must demonstrate Christian character by the way we live our lives. If you study these New Testament letters, all of these men taught the same thing. This is the template they set forth by the wisdom and leading of the Spirit of God and it is the template that we must follow.

# 18

# Conclusion

A few months ago I received what seemed to be a very credible check in the mail in the amount of $2400.00. Enclosed was a letter giving instructions on how to cash this check. The first step was to call the manager of this organization and then the other steps would be given. I called the number and the lady told me that the manager was out, but that all I needed to do was deposit the check and, once it cleared, pay a small fee.

I decided to do a little investigation on the internet. When I submitted the name and address, I found several things about this company. What struck me was one site that had posted a warning concerning this company and the money they professed to be giving out. As I read about all of the people who had done this, not one ever received the money. In fact, most of these people either lost the amount of the check or even more.

There are consequences for living a life that may seem to be Christian, but in all actuality is not. In the previous chapters we talked about the broad gate and how people seemed to enter that rather easily. Sometimes what seems to be a good thing actually is not. However, you cannot know unless you investigate to see if it is the real thing. John says, "Carefully weigh and examine what people tell you" (1 John 4:1 MSG). Paul tells the Corinthians, "Check up on yourselves. Are you really Christians? Do you pass the test? Do you feel Christ's presence and power more and more within you? Or are you just pretending to be Christians when actually you aren't at all?" ( 2 Cor. 13:5 TLB).

There are a lot of people claiming to be Christian and there are a lot of religious organizations that call themselves Christian. But are they? We need to do a little investigation as to whether they are or not. They may seem harmless, but the truth of the matter is that they are dangerous and they endanger the eternal lives of the innocent. We don't have to look far in our investigation as to the reality of this fact. In our lifetime we have seen those who have had the pretense of Christianity, but were devoid of the power and Person of the One who gives eternal life.

This is why we need to make sure we know, that we are confident that God is working in our lives. Paul says in his closing remarks of this section, "Brethren, join in following my example, and observe those who walk according to the pattern you have in us. For many walk, of whom I often told you, and now tell you even weeping, that they are enemies of the cross of Christ, whose end is destruction, whose god is their appetite, and whose glory is in their shame, who set their minds on earthly things. For our citizenship is in heaven, from which also we eagerly wait for a Savior, the Lord Jesus Christ; who will transform the body of our humble state into conformity with the body of His glory, by the exertion of the power that He has even to subject all things to Himself" (Phil. 3:17-21 NASB).

Paul's whole point here is that while the religious zealots were trying to push their own agenda, he was asking the Philippian Christians to follow his example. He had always cared for them and had been truthful with them. He was the real deal. His life was an open book for all to read. Without credible examples to follow, how are Christians to grow in the faith? While we are all responsible for our own spiritual growth, every one of us needs a mentor or an example to follow. We need to see it played out in real life.

The words, *join*, *follow*, and *example* are all found in one Greek word which means, "*imitator*." We are to have a singleness of mind and purpose along with the Apostle Paul. Our goal is to be like Christ, in every way and every day. Why? Because the consequences of depending on any system of theology that allows us to live in such a way, that is blatantly against the Word of God, leads to destruction.

That is exactly what worldly religions do when they reject the cross of Christ, when they form their own way to God. They basically encompass the mindset of the world which believes that anyone can achieve heaven by following their own understanding. In the end, however, they will only find destruction, a total separation from God.

The consequences of rejecting Jesus for self-effort will lead to the exclusion of heavenly citizenship. You cannot be a citizen of heaven if you are not grounded on the truth of the cross. The cross is God's way of bringing people into heaven. You may not like it. You may think it's cruel and distasteful, but so is sin and sin must be paid for. Jesus willingly gave His life for you and me. He didn't have to, He wanted to. The journey to joyful living goes through the cross. It has nothing to do with human effort, philosophies or denominational dogma.

There is another consequence that we must understand if we chose to reach heaven apart from Christ. If we are not watchful, if we are not focused, we could miss Jesus' coming again. Paul says that true Christian living is always mindful and watching for the return of Christ. We hold on to the things of this world loosely. We are not consumed by earthly things too passionately. John says, "The world is passing away, and also its lusts; but the one who does the will of God lives forever" (1 John 2:17 NASB).

Then, finally, Paul mentions in this last verse, " . . . the Lord Jesus Christ . . . will transform the body of our humble state into conformity with the body of His glory" (3:21). I cannot think of anything more wonderful than this, to know that the body we have here on earth will be replaced by one that is indestructible. Every one of us, as we get older, begins to experience the deterioration of our bodies. Every senior adult living today is a testimony to that fact. You and I cannot escape the inevitable. True Christians will not have to face the pain and the deterioration of these earthly bodies forever. We will have one that will last for eternity. The Bible tells us that God will remove all the pain and sorrow one day. He has fashioned a new body.

"And even we Christians, although we have the Holy Spirit within us as a foretaste of future glory, also groan to be released from pain and suffering. We, too, wait anxiously for that day when God will give us our full rights as his children, including the new bodies he has promised us—bodies that will never be sick again and will never die" (Rom. 8:23 TLB).

What about those who are not true believers, what happens to them? Well here is the last devastating consequence in trying to reach heaven on your own. My guess, **and this is just a guess**, is that not only will they live in eternal separation from God, but they will remain in their frail, weak bodies for eternity. If you think you have pain now, imagine what it would be like for an eternity? Listen, the price of getting it wrong at the end is too costly. It is my hope that if you are not sure about your eternal destiny, you make sure before you go any further. Let Jesus change your heart and let Him begin a good work in you.

# The Journey of Influence

## Philippians 4

# 19

# The Journey Of Faithfulness
# Philippians 4:1

Influence! What does that mean? What is "influence?" Well, think with me for a moment. Who has been the most influential person in your life? When you think of who you are and what you have become, who comes to mind about which you can say "I owe it all to _____!" Let's be real clear here, influence can be both good and bad. Your life and mine, to varying degrees, have been influenced with some good things and some bad things.

When we think of influential people we think of people like Abraham Lincoln, Martin Luther King Jr. and John F. Kennedy. There are people like Walt Disney, Elvis Presley, The Beatles and Michael Jackson. We could name some of the astronauts from throughout the years of space flight or professors from college or grade school. We could also name some of our relatives or parents. Each of these people has influenced us in some way or another. Well, is that good? That depends, were they worthy of emulation?

"*Influence*" is the power or ability to affect someone's beliefs or actions. Who we are and what we have become is largely due to the person or persons who have impacted our lives. We observed them throughout our lives and they, in some way, had an effect on how we lived, worked or believed. Again, you and I can be influenced either in a good way or a bad way.

On our last leg of this journey, Paul has once again issued a command for all of us, "Therefore . . . stand firm in the Lord" (4:1). What Paul is saying here is that we need to stand our ground. The word *"therefore"* is the rearview mirror of this journey. He is reaching back to what he has said and laying out the groundwork for what he wants to conclude with.

As with all of his other letters, Paul uses metaphors like the athlete and a soldier to describe the Christian life. He does this because these images always bring to mind the daily process of training, staying in shape and being alert. A soldier can't win a battle or persist in battle if he's not in shape. A soldier won't know the difference between a common villager and the enemy in the midst of the battle if he has not prepared for it. The same is true of an athlete. If he does not continually train, how will he be able to compete?

As Christians we also have to continue to grow spiritually. You remember Paul's previous words to us, "work out your salvation with fear and trembling" (2:12 NASB). The Christian life is not passive, but consists of daily action. To be a true Christian is not only a Sunday thing. To be a true Christian is a daily thing. Some have a tendency to take this Christian walk and reduce it to do's and don't's. This is why Paul gives this instruction to the Philippian church and to us to *"stand firm."*

This is the problem with the church today, especially in our country. We have lost that influential power in our homes, communities and in our government. We are seen as bigots, racists or terrorists. I must admit that I cannot put all the blame on nonbelievers for their assessment of the Christian life. Christians, as a whole, have not stood their ground. We have not fought the good fight. We continually show weakness in times of great concerns. In the last few years, we have as a Christian community, cowered to the political pressures and demands of anti-religious organizations. You can say what you want, but this is where we're at and we have a decision to make. We can remain on this same course of appeasing the popular ideas of the world or standing firm for the sake of the Gospel.

This is what Paul was fighting for when he wrote this letter to the Philippians. He saw how the religionists were coming in and persuading young churches to do it the "popular way." But it cannot be and we should not do it the popular way. We should stand firm on the truth of the Word and in the power of God's saving grace. So here, we are commanded to stand firm in the Lord.

Why should we stand firm in the Lord? There are several reasons why. First, it keeps us from developing wrong doctrinal beliefs. This was the problem of the Jewish sect. They felt that the externals were more important than having a relationship with Jesus. Once again, there are many denominations that teach the very same thing. They believe that actions are more important than redemption. They work hard for their faith, live by its dogma and, for the most part, are very sincere. However, they are lost according to the Scriptures because they have not had that change of heart. Pastor Rick Warren has a saying, "You can be sincere and be sincerely wrong."

True believers always consult the owner's manual, the Word of God. Paul calls the believer to, "Be diligent to present yourself approved to God as a workman who does not need to be ashamed, accurately handling the word of truth" (2 Tim. 2:15 NASB). The Apostle John tells us several times in his letters that he wrote these things so that we can know the life true believers are to live. Even Peter says, "This is now, beloved, the second letter I am writing to you in which I am stirring up your sincere mind by way of reminder, that you should remember the words spoken beforehand by the holy prophets and the commandment of the Lord and Savior spoken by your apostles" (2 Pet. 3:1-2 NASB).

Here's a second thing to consider, when we stand firm in the Lord it will keep us from falling into selfishness and wrong living. Paul talked about what Christianity is and what it is not in the previous chapters. He said true believers are not self-seekers. They are not out to get their way. True believers, according to Paul, are humble, serving and loving. They are not braggarts or deceitful. The Apostle Peter wrote, "Now for this very reason also, applying all diligence, in your faith supply moral excellence, and in your moral excellence, knowledge, and in your knowledge, self-control, and in your self-control, perseverance, and in your perseverance, godliness, and in your godliness, brotherly kindness, and in your brotherly kindness, love. For if these qualities are yours and are increasing, they render you neither useless nor unfruitful in the true knowledge of our Lord Jesus Christ" (2 Pet. 1:5-8 NASB).

Then, finally, being firmly grounded in the Lord will prevent us from being deceived and defeated by the devil. Paul wrote to the Ephesians, "Finally, be strong in the Lord and in the strength of His might. Put on the full armor of God, so that you will be able to stand firm against the schemes of the devil. For our struggle is not against flesh and blood, but against the rulers, against the powers, against the world forces of this darkness, against the spiritual forces of wickedness in the heavenly places" (Eph. 6:10-12 NASB).

So how do we stand firm? Paul says, "Therefore . . . in this way stand firm in the Lord." What way is he talking about? At the risk of being redundant he is saying that the way to be firmly grounded in the Lord is by what we have talked about in the previous section. Once again, the word *"therefore"* is the connecting idea of the previous chapter to this command "stand firm."

This is the way to stand firm. We need to make sure that we are standing firm in the Lord. I realize this is very basic, but we often have this tendency to forget the basics and wander off into wrong directions, beliefs or decisions. We are to stand firm *in the Lord.* That is the foundation upon which we must build. Paul tells the Corinthians that there is only one foundation upon which anyone can build and that is Jesus Christ (1 Cor. 3:11 NASB). The religionists of Paul's days were trying to build on the foundation of works and self-righteousness. They had determined how and what method was needed to reach God. Paul reminds the Corinthians that each man's work will be tested and in the end it will either stand the test or fail the test.

Listen, if your idea of Christianity is based on anything else but Jesus Christ, you will not pass the test. You and I cannot build a bridge to heaven on good efforts. We need to stop at this moment and truly ask ourselves if we really are building on the foundation of Jesus Christ or on the foundation of denominational membership. Eternity is too long to be wrong. As Christians, we have absolutely no excuse for not knowing how to live the Christian life. In the writings of the Apostles they always went back to the basics. They knew and had personally experienced that, as humans, we tend to forget the basics and revert back to bad habits, wrong beliefs and lifestyle.

The Apostle Paul tells us that if we are to stand firm in the Lord, we must always have the right blueprint for true Christian living. He said, " . . . having been built on the foundation of the apostles and prophets, Christ Jesus Himself being the corner stone" (Eph. 2:20 NASB). Standing firm in the Lord is not a matter of the external activity we do or pretend to do. It comes from knowing, trusting, and following the Lord Jesus Christ. Standing firm in Jesus comes when we know, when we are convinced that God is working in our lives. We are no longer the same. We are changing daily from one level of glory to another level of glory because of Jesus Christ.

Why is this so important? Why make a big deal about standing firm in the Lord? Isn't the fact that I go to church enough to show that I am a believer in God? A lot of people go to church and yet their very lives are contrary to the life of a true believer. People who live their lives in this manner not only have a misunderstanding of the Christian life, but also misrepresent the Christian life.

If we are going to influence our world, if we really want to see real change happen in our country, communities, and our churches, we need to be clear about the foundation upon which we build. Listen, the reputation of God is at stake here. God has entrusted us with a very prestigious position. As Paul has put it, "Therefore, we are ambassadors for Christ, as though God were making an appeal through us" (2 Cor. 5:20 NASB).

Our world today has mocked and even denied that there is a God simply because church people and denominational differences have presented a distorted image of the ever living, always loving Almighty God. Paul reprimanded the Jews for their arrogance and the hypocritical way they were living (Rom. 2:17-23). He tells them, "No wonder the Scriptures say that the world speaks evil of God because of you" (Rom. 2:24 TLB). Christians have not been as faithful either. We are equally responsible for the confusion in our world concerning God and Jesus Christ.

So, if we are going to influence those around us we must be sure, we must be convinced that Jesus Christ is living in us. We must live our Christian lives showing that He is alive and truly a part of our very being. Saying that we are Christians is not enough. Our words must match our actions. Paul says, "Do you not realize that you are a temple of God with the Spirit of God living in you?" (1 Cor. 3:16 NJB). The word "realize" carries the idea of having this certainty. John in his first Epistle uses the word *"know"* 38 times (NASB). He uses it because he realized that more often than we care to admit, we have a tendency to forget that the Christian life is a daily action. If we are not certain about this Christian life, then how is the world going to be convinced that God is real, that God loves, and that God is merciful? Paul told the Galatian Christians, "If we live by the Spirit, let us also walk by the Spirit" (Gal. 5:25 NASB).

A few years back, some of the staff members of one of the churches where I was serving as the Associate Pastor, went to a Saddleback conference in California. After one of the evening sessions, we really had nothing to do. After dinner we took a drive to see Robert Schuller's Crystal Cathedral. When we got there, the janitor let us in and we got to see the place where it all happens. I had only seen this place on TV and seeing it in person was just amazing. It was all glass. We could see everything. You might say it was very transparent.

"Transparency" is a very popular word today. Our government has made the proclamation that it would like to be the most transparent administration of the day. That is an admirable goal. This leads me to ask this question, "Are we, as Christians, truly transparent in our walk and talk?" The one thing that will make us less transparent is sin in our lives. As the called of God we cannot be double-minded or unstable in our ways as James tells us in his letter. John says we need to admit we have sin and ask for forgiveness. Listen, at the beginning I said that we are either influenced in good way or a bad way. Equally true is the fact that we are also an influence to others in either a good way or a bad way. As Christians we need to be salt and light to this world. So, what kind of an influential person are you?

> "If my people, who are called by my name,
> will humble themselves
> and pray and seek my face
> and turn from their wicked ways,
> then will I hear from heaven
> and will forgive their sin
> and will heal their land."
> 2 Chronicles 7:14 (NIV)

# 20

# The Journey Of Single-Mindedness
# Philippians 4:2-3

During my high school days I was involved in the orchestra, choir and ensemble. Not all at the same time, of course. On the weekends I would play football with other friends and neighbors. Later on in life I was involved in a Mariachi group and then in a contemporary Christian group. One of the things I discovered was that all of these activities needed one all-important element to achieve their purpose and goal. That one element was single-mindedness.

Without the element of single-mindedness, an orchestra will be just a bunch of instruments making indistinguishable noises. A football team will seem like a bunch of bumbling athletes. A choir will sound like a bunch of voices just trying to be heard above one another. None of these groups would be effective without single-mindedness. That is why there are coaches, choir directors, managers and team leaders. It keeps us focused on the purpose. In the Christian life, Jesus Christ is the coach, the manager, the choir director of our lives. Without Him, we will be disorganized and purposeless. That is why Paul tells us, "Join with others in following my example, brothers, and take note of those who live according to the pattern we gave you." Phil. 3:17 NIV).

How do we influence our world? We do it first by glorifying the Lord Jesus Christ through the life we are living. Paul says, *"stand firm in the Lord."* When we do this, we show or testify to this world that God is alive and active in our world and especially in our lives. This is not just a single person activity. If we claim that we are in the body of Christ, then we need to show it by our singleness of mind. The perception we have given to this world is that there are many different gods and, therefore, there are different ways to reach heaven.

Paul has already told us that we need to follow his example and others who have walked in this same manner (Phil. 3:17). There are numerous references where believers are commanded by the Apostles to be "imitators" either of them or of God (1 Cor. 4:16&11:1; Eph. 5:1; 1 Thess.1:6 &2:14;). Paul tells Timothy, "What you heard from me, keep as the pattern of sound teaching, with faith and love in Christ Jesus" (2 Tim. 1:13 NIV). Paul tells the Ephesian Christians, "Consequently, you are no longer foreigners and aliens, but fellow citizens with God's people and members of God's household, built on the foundation of the apostles and prophets, with Christ Jesus himself as the chief cornerstone" (Eph. 2:19-20 NIV). He said that any foundation they build on must have Jesus Christ as the cornerstone. This was a fundamental truth of the Apostles and the prophets. He also says that, when we build on this foundation, then we are "fellow citizens with God's people and members of God's household."

Holy Scripture teaches us that the body of Christ does not exist in the form of denominational titles, dogma or philosophies, but on Jesus Christ and His Word. John says, "Whoever claims to live in him must walk as Jesus did" (1 John 2:6 NIV). As Christians, we are not of this family or that family, but of the same family if we have the Spirit of God living in us. So we must, as Christians, agree on the essentials. God is the one true God and salvation is through Jesus Christ. Anyone wanting to be a part of the family of God must come through Jesus Christ. We are not saved by water or by man-made religious precepts, but by the blood of Jesus Christ. There is but one God manifested in three personalities not three separate persons. We cannot obtain salvation through Mary, the mother of Jesus. It is only through the cross of Christ that we find forgiveness. This is the pattern we must hold on to. This is what the Apostles taught.

One of the most common excuses for not coming to Jesus from unbelievers is "Which church is right? Which god is the true god? Who is actually right?" I must confess that I certainly don't blame them for their refusal to see the truth of the Gospel and the power of God. Christians need to live with the certainty that God is truly working in their lives. We also need to be convinced of the truth of the Gospel message. Paul tells us to preach the Word. There can only be one message, not many. The way I see it and have learned from experience is that the Gospel message is Jesus Christ and Him crucified.

Being a Christian is not something we need to keep quiet about either. We're not in a secret society like some have made it. Being a Christian is like being an ambassador for God and ambassadors speak out for the one they represent. They have a message, not of their own, but from the one who has sent them. Paul tells the Corinthians, "When we tell you these things, we do not use words that come from human wisdom. Instead, we speak words given to us by the Spirit, using the Spirit's words to explain spiritual truths" (1 Cor. 2:13 NLT). He also tells the Thessalonian Christians, "So then, brethren, stand firm and hold to the traditions which you were taught, whether by word of mouth or by letter from us" (2 Thess. 2:15 NASB).

So, in order to be an influence in this world we must have singleness of mind concerning God and His Word. We must also be truthful in our love for one another. Paul says, "My beloved brethren whom I long to see, my joy and crown" (4:1). I am sure you have heard this saying many times, "Christians are the only ones that shoot their wounded." Funny how we always seem to justify the way we treat each other in the church. Here Paul addresses these believers as *brethren, my joy and crown*. What does he mean here? He is demonstrating love and concern for them. This is not some self-manufactured type of affection. He was genuinely concerned about them and that is why he sent Epaphroditus and Timothy to them.

He also had a longing for them. He craved, if you please, their fellowship and affection. You see, true love always longs to be with the ones you love. Jesus said, "A new command I give you: Love one another. As I have loved you, so you must love one another. By this all men will know that you are my disciples, if you love one another" (John 13:34-35 NIV). That is the purpose of demonstrating love to each other, "All men will know that you are my disciples." Who wants to join a church where they are treated with indifference? John says, "Dear friends, let us love one another, for love comes from God. Everyone who loves has been born of God and knows God" (1 John 4:7 NIV).

Paul also says they were his joy. He took pride in them. He was, in a sense, honored to be identified with them. This is not really the picture of the church today. I know that some put on the pretense of being happy with one another, but let's be real truthful here, some of the time we are not. We see each other and give the standard "How are you doing?" greeting never fully intending to listen to the response. You don't think that's true? Next time you're at church and someone says, "How are you doing?" wait and see if they stop long enough to listen to what you have to say.

There should also be pride in the fellowship you belong to. Are you sincerely proud of your ministry at your church? Here's how you can tell if you are truly proud and honored to be in a fellowship such as yours. How often do you invite someone to it? Not just to your special services like Easter and Christmas, but your on-going services? A few years back, Gayla and I served at a church here in town. It seemed to be a good place to worship until all of the little hidden demons started to come out. There was so much turmoil there that we were ashamed to invite people and we certainly didn't want to tell them where we went to church.

Finally, Paul says they were his "crown." The Philippians were proof of the extraordinary work of God through his ministry. The word "crown" in the Greek refers to a wreath as opposed to a crown a king might wear. The wreath was given to the victor in the athletic events of Paul's day. Here we could look at the wreath as God's blessing on the ministry of Paul. It was his reward for the effort and commitment he had to the Gospel. We live in a time when people are really looking for something that is real and that gives them hope for a better tomorrow. This is the ideal time for true believers to start living and acting like the children of God.

If we are going to be influential in our communities where we live and interact with others, then we need to be united in purpose. Paul addresses one of the main problems in the church at Philippi. He specifically identifies two individuals. He says, "I urge Euodia and I urge Syntyche to live in harmony in the Lord" (4:2 NASB). These two prominent women in the church were at odds with each other. Such disunity in the body of Christ can and does create divisions and exclusion.

Not long ago two prominent TV preachers were at odds with each other. Each of these men was accusing the other of wrongdoing. This was being played out in the national media while a lost world was looking at and reading or hearing this foolishness. The media loves it when there is religious feuding. However, it serves no purpose when it concerns the Gospel message.

Paul urged Euodia and Syntyche to live in harmony in the Lord. The word "harmony" basically means "to be of the same mind." Disunity will rob a church of its power and of its testimony. The doctrine can be as sound as ever, but if the heart is wrong sound doctrine will be of no use. I am not saying that we have to agree on everything. I know that is impossible. In any church there must be this mindset that we are not here for ourselves. We represent a higher power. We are ambassadors for Christ.

To the Corinthians Paul says, "Now I exhort you, brethren, by the name of our Lord Jesus Christ, that you all agree and that there be no divisions among you, but that you be made complete in the same mind and in the same judgment" (1 Cor. 1:10 NASB). The Apostle Peter reiterates Paul's command when he says, "Finally, all of you, live in harmony with one another; be sympathetic, love as brothers, be compassionate and humble" (1 Pet. 3:8 NIV).

As Christians we are called upon to live a different way. We are new creations and our actions and our lives need to reflect that. If we are going to change the world, if we are going to be an influence in this world, then we need to exemplify that through our daily lives. This letter was written for all Christians. If there is going to be singleness of mind and purpose, then it begins with Jesus changing us from the inside out. Without His love in us we will not be able to love others. If we are not able to love others, then certainly we will not be able to agree with each other. All of the pettiness will supersede any good intentions we may have. That is why Paul says we must have the conviction that God is working in our lives.

This leads me to one final consideration and that is, when we have that singleness of mind, we will work together in unity. Paul goes on to say, "Indeed, true companion, I ask you also to help these women who have shared my struggle in the cause of the gospel, together with Clement also and the rest of my fellow workers, whose names are in the book of life" (4:2-3 NASB). Christians should exemplify unity in effort. As I said before we are now of a different mindset because of this new life we have in Christ. What we do for the sake of the Gospel is done in unity of purpose.

Paul truly has a pastor's heart. Even though he singled out these two women and called them to live with singleness of mind, he also gave them recognition. He brought to the forefront their efforts in helping him in the ministry of the Gospel. He also asked that those in the Philippian church continue to help them as well. This was important to Paul and this should be important to us. We are citizens of a new world.

But what does Paul mean when he says, "my fellow workers, whose names are in the book of life." Just like we are registered in our country, showing proof that we are citizens of the United States, so our names are recorded in God's book of life showing we are citizens of a heavenly kingdom. When we travel to a different country, people in that country know that we are a US citizen by the way we talk and act. They recognize the place and the culture of our country.

The body of Christ, the local church, is God's only way to show the world that He exists and that He loves and cares for them. Here's the problem, the church has not lived up to its purpose. The body of Christ, of which we are members, has shown at times to be exclusive and childish. That is the image the world has coming from many of our churches today. We have not represented the kingdom of God in a very positive way.

Again, Christians are the body of Christ. It makes no difference what we call ourselves. If we have been born again, baptized in the name of the Father, Son and Holy Spirit, if we truly seek to bring Him glory, and if we proclaim the Gospel of the Apostles, then we are the children of God. In the past God used the Jewish nation to proclaim His glory. Today He is using the church to do the same. Shame on us for belittling the glory of God for our own pettiness and selfish motives. We are called upon to be fellow workers and true companions.

> "Speak the truth in love, growing in every way
> more and more like Christ,
> who is the head of his body, the church.
> He makes the whole body fit together perfectly.
> As each part does its own special work,
> it helps the other parts grow, so that the whole body
> is healthy and growing and full of love."
> (Eph. 4:15-16 NLT)

# 21

# The Journey Of Example
# Philippians 4:4-9

Have you ever tried to put something together without the proper instructions? Sometimes we have the idea that we really don't need to have instructions, all we need are the proper tools and some brains. What happens when we can't really figure it out on our own? We read the instructions! As we read the instructions we also look at the picture. I find that reading the instructions and looking at the picture has saved me a lot of time and hair.

That is what Paul is saying here when he says, "The things you have learned and received and heard and seen in me, practice these things, and the God of peace will be with you" (Phil. 4:9 NASB). Now, I have purposely begun with this verse so that we can see how Paul says we should practice the Christian life. This is like reading the instructions we have been given and also looking at the example of how those instructions are to look in the life of the believer. Paul in his other writings tells us that he stood as an example for believers to follow.

He tells the Corinthians, "Follow my example, as I follow the example of Christ; Therefore I urge you to imitate me." Once again to the Philippians he says, "Join with others in following my example, brothers, and take note of those who live according to the pattern we gave you." To Timothy his faithful friend he writes, "Don't let anyone look down on you because you are young, but set an example for the believers in speech, in life, in love, in faith and in purity." Finally, John writes to the believers in his care, "My dear friend, never follow a bad example, but keep following the good one; whoever does what is right is from God, but no one who does what is wrong has ever seen God." (cf. 1 Cor. 11:1; 4:16; Phil. 3:17; 1 Tim. 4:12 NIV; 3 Jn. 1:11 NJB)

Paul is saying that we are to set the example, not only for other believers, but for a lost world. What hope can there be for anyone if Jesus is not real? What purpose does the body of believers serve if it is not to show the world that Jesus is alive and active in our lives? When we look at this letter to the Philippians we find that we are more than just members in a church. Paul says that we are to be examples. There should be no shame in this and there should be no fear in this. If we are learning, living, listening and doing, then we are capable of being examples for a lost and dying world.

That is what Paul says in this ninth verse, "The things you have learned and received and heard and seen in me, practice these things." The word "practice" carries the idea of something that is ongoing. When you hear of a doctor or lawyer having a practice it means that it is a continuous profession. That is what the believer is encouraged to do here, to have a daily walk, a 24/7 interaction with God. Jesus said, "If any of you wants to be my follower, you must turn from your selfish ways, take up your cross daily, and follow me" (Luke 9:23 NLT). This is where a lot of us get into trouble and end up in a ditch at some point during our journey to joy. It seems to me that Christianity has been reduced to doing this or believing that instead of living the life. It has become more mechanical and less personal.

As Christians, most of us know more than we practice. We have a lot of head knowledge but very little practical experience. We sit in Bible study after Bible study and gain all of this information, but there is little transformation or, for that matter, no transformation. I am that way. I get a little head knowledge, a new insight and I think I have more spiritual smarts than the guy sitting in the back pew. What I have discovered about myself is that I am prone to take this information and wear it as a new suit rather than applying what I have learned in my daily living. That is not living the Christian life. Living the Christian life is practicing what we are learning on a daily basis. John the Baptist said of himself, "I must decrease but He must increase." That is living the Christian life daily.

So Paul begins to lay out for us how to live the Christian life. In other words, here is how we are to be examples for other believers, but more specifically, for a lost and dying world. He says in verse four, "Rejoice in the Lord always; again I will say, rejoice!" Now we have talked about this issue of "joy" in chapter 13, but I want to make some additional comments about this here. Paul says that we are to rejoice in the Lord always. As you have come to realize, this letter is about maintaining true Christian joy. There were a lot of things that had caused a loss of joy in these new believers. Paul's fear was that if they did not have the proper perspective of joy in their lives, they would continue to disintegrate as a community.

So Paul says that we are to "Rejoice . . . always" and then he repeats it again. Why? Well, you and I know from experience that we are not always able to rejoice. Sometimes it is really hard to find that sense of joy in our lives. Now, while this may be true, Paul says that we are still to rejoice. How is this possible? One of the things we like to do in order to give the perception that we are joyful, is to approach our unwanted circumstances with indifference. We think that by stuffing all of our feelings within ourselves we can appear to be joyful. Paul isn't advocating for us to ignore these difficult situations. Paul isn't advocating this attitude of "I am not going to let these hard times get me down." That would be foolish and ineffective. It's also not the way the Gospel tells us to face life.

Paul says that true rejoicing comes from the Lord. Here again we are brought back to the central theme that he continually gives us. The true believer finds his life, power, and direction in the Lord. Does this mean we are to just laugh at what we are going through? No! Joy is living life in Jesus no matter what circumstance we may be facing. I don't find it very easy to be joyful when facing a major illness. I find no humor in very trying times. The fact that I may be facing these things, though, cannot prevent me from being joyful in the Lord. When I base my joy and confidence in Jesus, when I am learning, living and listening to the Spirit of God, then no matter what I am facing I can rest in this attitude of joy.

Joy is not a manufactured human emotion. There are some things that can give us the appearance of this happiness, but in the end those things we depend on soon lose that power. Human happiness goes only so far and then it ends. That is why people are often unhappy in their situations and are constantly looking for things to give them happiness. If our joy is anchored in the Lord, then we find satisfaction and ultimately peace in our lives.

That is why Paul encouraged Euodia and Syntyche to live in harmony in the Lord. When our joy is based on Jesus then it really doesn't matter if things get done our way or if our opinion is honored. When we are in harmony with God, we are in harmony with each other. Here is one of the reasons we lose this attitude of joy in our lives. We are out of fellowship with the Lord. We are more concerned about getting our way than getting along or moving in the same direction.

One final thing about rejoicing in the Lord. When our joy is firmly grounded in the Lord, no matter what circumstances we may be facing at any particular moment, we are able to face them with courage and hope. When we are able to live a life like that, then it is an example to a lost world that there is someone greater than our situations who can give us hope for tomorrow. People in our world today need someone greater than their situations. They are looking for something to give them that hope and that peace in their lives. A Christian who is miserable, who is constantly complaining and critical, is a bad example and has a wrong understanding of the Christian life and of Biblical doctrine. When the world looks at people like this, they see no reason for Jesus in their lives. So we are commanded to rejoice in the Lord.

Not only are we to rejoice in the Lord, we are called to, "Let your (our) gentle spirit be known to all men. The Lord is near" (4:5 NASB). The word "gentle" can mean a variety of things. Most scholars define it as, generosity, goodwill, friendliness, charity toward the faults of others, mercy toward the failures of others, bigheartedness, moderation, forbearance, and gentleness. I rather like Dr. Lloyd Jones' definition, "Control of oneself and one's spirit, and is shown by self-control, self mastery, possession of one's spirit and of one's activity" (Lloyd-Jones, D. Martyn. *The Life of Peace*, Philippians 3 and 4, 2nd ed. Grand Rapids: Baker Book House, 1993, pg 157). He says it basically means that a true believer is never so determined to get their own way that they fail to see the damage or misrepresentation it is causing the Gospel. True believers are mindful of how their attitudes and opinions affect the world around them.

Here, in this last chapter Paul urged and even pleaded with these two women, Euodia and Syntyche, to agree in the Lord. It seems that they were easily offended in their desires and opinions. So Paul calls upon them to agree in the Lord. Listen, when we are truly living in an active daily walk with Jesus, we will not give into these selfish desires of getting our way. You may recall my comment on people who approach the body of Christ with the Burger King mentality, you want it your way.

Here, Paul is saying that the true believer acts and reacts in a gentle or self-controlled way. True believers are not easily offended. Paul is a good example of this and he tells us to imitate his example. He was in prison and there were those who were trying to embarrass him and even ridiculed him. How does he respond? "Some, to be sure, are preaching Christ even from envy and strife . . . the former proclaim Christ out of selfish ambition rather than from pure motives, thinking to cause me distress in my imprisonment. What then? Only that in every way, whether in pretense or in truth, Christ is proclaimed; and in this I rejoice. Yes, and I will rejoice" (Phil. 1:15-18 NASB).

Paul always looked at his life in light of the Gospel message. Unfortunately the body of Christ today has given conflicting messages concerning the truth of the Gospel. Here we are reminded once again that the Gospel is something that is living and active. It is not just some black ink on white pages. It is something that is real and visible to anyone. That is why Peter says, "But in your hearts set apart Christ as Lord. Always be prepared to give an answer to everyone who asks you to give the reason for the hope that you have. But do this with gentleness and respect" (1 Pet. 3:15 NIV). This will seem unlikely if we constantly give the impression that there are a variety of ways to get into heaven.

Self-control also allows us to see others and their needs. The believer that is able to control his spirit, actions and attitudes is also willing to see why certain people react the way they do. One of the greatest ministries I was involved in was the Celebrate Recovery ministry developed by the Saddleback Church. This ministry was built on understanding and acceptance. It was designed to not only give help and guidance but also encouragement through the Gospel of grace. One cannot serve in a ministry like this unless there is genuine love and concern for the needs of others. It has taught me to look at others with a more loving eye, rather than with an attitude of legalism. This is why Paul says, "Indeed, true companion, I ask you also to help these women who have shared my struggle in the cause of the gospel" (4:3). Euodia and Syntyche needed encouragement, not retribution.

If you know anything about Paul, you know that his life as a new believer was not without some controversy. Early in the ministry of Paul and Barnabas, there was disagreement about John Mark going with them on a missionary journey. Paul did not want to take this young man because earlier John Mark deserted them and had not continued in the work. But Barnabas felt strongly about John Mark and because of this Paul and Barnabas parted company (cf. Acts 15:36-38). I want you to notice how Paul grows in Christian maturity. In his letter to Timothy he writes, "Only Luke is with me. Pick up Mark and bring him with you, for he is useful to me for service" (2 Tim. 4:11 NASB). Paul has come to see the value in a person because he has grown in his love for Christ.

I've had the pleasure of meeting and having conversations with David Meece. David is one of the most popular Christian singer/songwriters of our time. What is so unique about David is his testimony. He exemplifies true Christian character. He tells about how he struggled with a certain situation in his life long after he became a Christian. Years later when he turns everything about this situation to God he learns what it means to be understanding and forgiving. Listening to David share his life I saw how intimately God is involved in the believer's life.

Now, I have belabored this thought simply because as the body of Christ we have been more inclined to build up walls of animosity over nonessentials and have disregarded the essentials. Christians spend more time worrying about performance rather than process. We want to live or die on philosophies which lead nowhere and are usually built on misguided doctrine. But the Christian life is one of practice. Paul says we are to work out our salvation, we are to follow the example of other true believers, we are to heed the words of sound doctrine, and we are to be convinced that God is working in our lives.

Another characteristic of true believers is contentment. Paul says, "Be anxious for nothing, but in everything by prayer and supplication with thanksgiving let your requests be made known to God" (4:6 NASB). To "Be anxious for nothing" reveals a flaw in the Christian life which should not exist. We are fond of saying that we walk by faith but, when unwanted circumstances appear, is that still our conviction? I say that because it is always easier to make a statement than to live out that statement. When I was diagnosed with cancer, my first reaction was not one of faith but of fear. I was anxious rather than trusting.

It happens, I am sure, to a lot of believers. In this time of great financial instability in our world nothing is more evident than the anxiousness of people. But as Christians we are called upon to reflect this new way of living. We are commanded not to be anxious, not to live with this worrisome characteristic. For a Christian to be anxious, worried, or fearful is once again a misunderstanding of the Christian life and the doctrine we proclaim to believe in.

In order to avoid such an error as anxiousness in our lives, we must consider what is meant by this. To avoid this worrisome fear we cannot just stop and say "I am not going to worry about anything." That would be foolish because, no matter how hard I try not to worry, my mind will constantly be focused on the thing I am not to worry about.

Listen, the problem that is presented here is not one that can easily be remedied by the things we are taught such as, do not worry, or worry doesn't accomplish anything, or to worry will not change the situation. And while that is true and seems quite logical, what we fail to see is the heart of the problem. I've heard many preachers including my former pastor, Pastor Ron Hart, say "The heart of the human problem is the problem of the human heart." That is what is at stake here—our hearts and minds. To enforce some psychological remedy on the heart is useless. Only something greater than willpower or modern psychology can cure the problem. And here Paul says, "Do not be anxious for anything" and then he gives us the remedy, "let your requests be made known to God." That is the answer or, if you will, the cure for an anxious heart. Talk with God, communicate with God, and trust in His process.

How to do we do this? Well, Paul gives us three things to do in an anxious situation, "In everything by prayer and supplication with thanksgiving let your requests be made known to God." First, he says we are to pray. Before you go out and fall to your knees and begin to pray, you need to understand what Paul is saying here. It is characteristic of Christians when faced with the potential of an anxious heart to run to God, fall on our knees, and begin to beg for release. That is not what Paul is advocating here. He is saying, that when faced with this anxiousness, we need to come and worship. That is the idea here. To worship God.

That is what Isaiah did. It says, "In the year of King Uzziah's death I saw the Lord sitting on a throne, lofty and exalted, with the train of His robe filling the temple" (Isa. 6:1 NASB). Notice what is not present in his worship. Uzziah had died and the people were without a king and protector and yet that is not mentioned in his prayer. Isaiah saw the Lord and He was still on the throne.

This is what is lost in most prayer seminars. They give us the mechanics of prayer, but they never mention the worship that must exist in prayer. Prayer must focus on God and His power and glory. Prayer must never begin with our problems but with praise and adoration for the great and awesome God. We need to lay aside our difficulties and focus on Him. Do we see the Lord high and lifted up? We sing about it, but do we live it? David, in his writings, says over and over "Praise the Lord." Here was a guy who faced great difficulties in his life and yet he praised God in all things.

It is only after we have truly spent our time in worship that we bring our concerns to God. We cannot really expect to have God listen to our request if we truly don't see Him as high and lifted up. Our concerns and requests will seem pointless if we do not see God as capable or powerful to do something about them. This leads us to this last thought. We come to Him in thanksgiving. We must recognize the goodness of God. We must have that certainty that He is for us and not against us. We must realize that the things we are facing, are not because of His doing, but because we live in a fallen world. If we are not grateful then why would He honor our requests? We need to thank Him in advance for who He is, what He has done for us, and what He needs to do in our lives.

Now, Paul gives us the promise in all of this, "And the peace of God, which surpasses all comprehension, will guard your hearts and your minds in Christ Jesus" (4:7 NASB). Peace is the opposite of anxiousness. When we worship the Lord, communicate the things facing our lives, and thank Him for His goodness no matter what He answers, we have peace. In other words, we have this contentment in our hearts. While the world may be in this chaotic state we are not anxious because we are trusting in God's power and purpose.

You see, God's power is unlimited and transcends all human effort and solutions. And this power is able to act as a sentry for our hearts and minds. Here again, it is the heart and mind that needs that stability. There are a variety of things that press upon us and push us towards this anxious state. But this peace of God, this tranquility of mind, protects us when faced with uncertainty.

Then finally, all of this is done *"In Christ Jesus."* None of this is possible without the intervention of Jesus Christ. You and I cannot create this peace in our hearts and minds. Something greater than ourselves must influence us. This is why Paul could face all of the hardships of life. This is why he could say, "For me to live is Christ and to die is gain."

He saw the Lord high and exalted. When he prayed it was not for some immediate relief of his situation, but for the release of the Gospel in his life. You and I tend to pray with the assumption that God must act and must act immediately to remove the thorn from our side.

However, God is not at all bound to answer us a certain way or for any reason. His way of dealing with our situation is that He may let it go on no matter how difficult and uncertain our futures will be. His only responsibility is to continue to perfect us. This again is why Paul could say, "I am convinced of this very thing, that He who began a good work in you will perfect it until the day of Jesus Christ." God is more interested in our character than our comfort as Pastor Rick [Warren] is fond of saying.

Paul concludes this section with a final exhortation. He says that if we are to rest in the peace of God, and if we are to experience true joy in our lives, then we must meditate on these principles. Not only are we to meditate on them, they must influence our daily lives as well. He says, "Finally, brethren, whatever is true, whatever is honorable, whatever is right, whatever is pure, whatever is lovely, whatever is of good repute, if there is any excellence and if anything worthy of praise, dwell on these things" (4:8 NASB).

The life of the believer must not only consist of right living, but also must accurately represent the Lord Jesus Christ. That means, we must hold on to the truth of the Gospel. We not only have the information, but also have a transformation taking place in our lives. Then, believers must live a life that is just, thinking on things of a righteous nature. The things that would please God are the things upon which we need to dwell. Along with that believers are encouraged to think of things that are pure. These are things that are morally clean or things that are not sinful. The whole thought process and actions of the believer must be pleasing to God and worthy of respect from those outside of the body of Christ. We are, in a sense, controlled by the very life of the Lord Jesus Christ. And that is what the world needs to see.

Why? Well, Paul says because *"the Lord is near."* No one knows when Jesus will return. We know, as believers, that He will return, but when that will happen is not for us to know. But what we do know is that the presence of the Lord is always near. Jesus is as near to the believer as anyone can be. He knows our hurts and sees our struggles. His presence assures us of the power we have to make it through this life. And being convinced of this, and living our lives with that conviction, we can enjoy the peace of God as we walk through this journey.

> "But in all these things we overwhelmingly
> conquer through Him who loved us.
> For I am convinced that neither death,
> nor life, nor angels, nor principalities, nor things present,
> nor things to come, nor powers, nor height, nor depth,
> nor any other created thing,
> will be able to separate us from the love of God,
> which is in Christ Jesus our Lord."
> Romans 8:37-39 (NASB)

# 22

# The Journey Of Contentment
# Philippians 4:10-18

Nowhere is contentment more lacking than in the lives of people in our world today. We all remember Katrina? It was the deadliest storm to have hit America in several years. Two women who had been living in this area found themselves displaced and being evacuated to New Mexico and Texas. When they were allowed to return to their neighborhoods, they found their homes uninhabitable. You would think they would have been discouraged, maybe angry, or even resentful. But instead these two women found a way to bring joy and contentment to their lives in the midst of a great tragedy.

Upon their return, they became involved with helping others. They volunteered to start and oversee a clinic and one of them even gave up her home for the new clinic. They took a bad situation and made the most of it by helping others. They saw what they had and used it looking beyond their own misery. I can't think of a better example than these two women who exemplify contentment in the midst of such uncertainties.

That is where we find Paul. In his final remarks to the Philippian Christians he gives us his example of true contentment. As I said before, Paul's life was centered on this one belief, "For I am confident of this very thing, that He who began a good work in you will perfect it until the day of Christ Jesus" (1:6). This is the guiding force in his life. In Jesus he finds this contentment. He knows and trusts by experience that

God is looking out for his best interest no matter what the circumstances may be.

So once again he reiterates his basis for finding true contentment in his situations. He says, "I can do all things through Him who strengthens me." (Phil. 4:13 NASB). When we live a life centered in Christ, Christ gives us the power to live out our lives no matter what we are facing. It shouldn't be this mentality that some Christians have of just "*enduring life.*"

Looking at some people who call themselves Christians and we see a face that looks like Eeyore from Winnie the Pooh. We can almost hear them say, "I guess I have to endure the lot that God has given me." They act as if God intentionally gives them this miserable life. We live in a fallen world and things in this world are not equal or fair. I know that our political leaders spend time and effort trying to make everything equal and fair for everyone, but that is not humanly possible. There are inadequacies in this world simply because of sin, human arrogance, and selfishness.

So Paul's answer to these unwanted circumstances was not to whine about them but to trust God through it. He says, "I can do all things," in other words, "I can face all of these uncertainties and struggles," by this, "through Him who empowers me." That is the definition of strength, *empowerment*. Notice he doesn't say "I can do all things by just biting my lip and enduring these circumstances." It is by depending on the power that is in Christ. He tells the Corinthians, "Therefore I am well content with weaknesses, with insults, with distresses, with persecutions, with difficulties, for Christ's sake; for when I am weak, then I am strong" (2 Cor. 12:10 NASB).

So he tells the Philippians that he rejoiced in the fact that they were concerned about him and had made a sacrifice to provide for his needs. Paul was grateful for their love and concern. But he quickly inserted this comment concerning their gift, "Not that I speak from want, for I have learned to be content in whatever circumstances I am. I know how to get along with humble means, and I also know how to live in prosperity; in any and every circumstance I have learned the secret of being filled and going hungry, both of having abundance and suffering need" (4:11-12 NASB).

I want us to understand that just because we are Christians or Christian leaders working in some church ministry it does not gives us the right to demand or expect anything from anyone. Paul was neither expecting this gift nor did he tell them they needed to give the gift. The gift was totally a gift of love and sacrifice from their heart. They were thankful for Paul and his ministry. As Christians, we need to have a humble and gracious heart. People should be free to give or not to give. We cannot force people to be giving people. Giving is a grateful response to God for what He has done and is doing in our lives and in the lives of those who serve us. These two ladies that I mentioned at the beginning gave because of a grateful heart for what had been done for them. But they also saw a need in the lives of others and they gave of themselves based on that need.

This is what the Philippian Christians had done for Paul. They were not forced to give or made to feel guilty for not giving. They gave because of a grateful heart. I've been in churches where the plea is always about the money we do not have or get from our members. Some go out of their way to make others feel guilty for not giving or not giving enough. In my younger years before I became a Christian, I was raised in the Catholic church. I was always amazed at how many times they passed the basket in one service. Even in some Protestant churches they pass the plate around as many times as it takes to get the amount.

We need, as believers, to have a different way of looking at circumstances. Paul says he had "learned to be content in whatever circumstances." That is the process of the Christian life—learning and growing in Jesus. To experience contentment means we have to learn God's way of living life and to trust in Him on a daily basis. As believers we need to rise above what the world says brings contentment. For Paul, he had learned the secret, that power, of an intimate relationship with Christ. The writer of Hebrews tells us, "Make sure that your character is free from the love of money, being content with what you have; for He Himself has said, 'I will never desert you, nor will I ever forsake you'" (Heb. 13:5 NASB). This is another way of saying what Paul has told us previously, "He who began a good work in you will perfect it . . ." (1:6).

Paul tells us that in his life he had experienced a variety of circumstances. He says, "I know how to get along with humble means, and I also know how to live in prosperity; in any and every circumstance I have learned the secret of being filled and going hungry, both of having abundance and suffering need" (4:12 NASB). You see, in this life we are not always going to be on a high mountain. There will be times when we will have to walk through some valleys. You may be financially set but there could come a time when you will lose what you have. Or you may not have enough money to meet your everyday expenses.

Life for many Americans today has radically changed in this last year. Some who had a nice home, a good job or money to do a variety of things have lost much in this recession. There is no denying that life is really hard for many people. But for the Christian today when faced with these circumstances can we say with Paul, "I know how to get along with humble means, and I also know how to live in prosperity; in any and every circumstance I have learned the secret of being filled and going hungry, both of having abundance and suffering need?"

Do you know the secret to contentment? Paul tells us that this secret is something we learn and we learn it by living daily with Jesus Christ. Our hope, the Christian hope is based on a Person and not on property or prosperity. True rejoicing results from learning the secret of contentment. Proverbs 19:23 says, "The fear of the LORD leads to life: Then one rests content, untouched by trouble." In other words, what I believe the writer is saying is that when we find our contentment in Christ, whatever may be taking place in our lives will not bring discouragement, bitterness, anger, complaining or indifference. We can truly say along with Paul, "I can do all things through Him who strengthens me."

D. Martyn Lloyd-Jones wrote, "The secret of power is to discover and to learn from the New Testament what is possible for us in Christ. What I have to do is to go to Christ. I must spend my time with Him. I must meditate upon Him, I must get to know Him. That was Paul's ambition—*'that I might know Him.'* I must maintain my contact and communion with Christ and I must concentrate on knowing Him . . . I must read the Bible, I must exercise, I must practice the Christian life, I must live the Christian life in all its fullness." (Spiritual Depression: Its Causes and Cure, Grand Rapids: Eerdmans, 1965, pg. 298-99)

Paul concludes his thoughts on contentment by using the illustration of the Philippians' generosity to him in his ministry. He says, "Nevertheless, you have done well to share with me in my affliction. You yourselves also know, Philippians, that at the first preaching of the gospel, after I left Macedonia, no church shared with me in the matter of giving and receiving but you alone; for even in Thessalonica you sent a gift more than once for my needs." (4:14-16 NASB). These Philippian Christians demonstrated their love for God and Paul by giving sacrificially. Paul didn't seek for the gift, they did this on their own.

Christianity is living a life that is selfless. It does not seek for glory or attention but is moved by compassion and concern. The problem with the Christian church today is that it has become more of a business than a ministry. I realize that in a time of financial distress people do not give generously. I understand that. I also realize that churches are very mindful of the monies they receive and the responsibilities they have to meet their daily operational expenses. But what concerns me most is that some inexcusably use these circumstances to cut back on giving to greater needs around our communities and around our world.

I have seen churches refuse to give anything to their participating associations or districts simply because they didn't bring in as much or felt that it was more prudent to put it in a bank somewhere for safe-keeping. That I believe is selfishness. I am reminded of something Pastor Rick Warren taught sometime back. He said, "When in need, plant a seed." Pastor Rick looked beyond what they had to what they could do. He didn't see the amount at hand, but the potential of God at work.

That is what the Philippians believed and did and that is what the young ladies I spoke about at the beginning did as well. They took the seed of generosity and planted it in a place of great need. These women, like these Christians at Philippi, didn't have much, if anything, at all. But what they did have was faith. Paul says that not only did they give to his ministry efforts several times, but they were the only ones that gave. The writer of Proverbs says, "One who is gracious to a poor man lends to the Lord, And He will repay him for his good deed" (Prov. 19:17 NASB).

Generosity is an outcome of a contented heart. When we are firmly rooted in our relationship with Jesus and we find our contentment and fulfillment in Him then we are free to give and to give generously. This is proof of a Christian life. This is what demonstrates that we have fully trusted in Him and are convinced that He is doing a good work in us. The Philippian Christians exemplified that in their giving. Paul didn't need or require that all churches give to him. In fact, he was so mindful of the Gospel that at times he would raise his own support simply because he didn't want people thinking he was out to get rich from these poor struggling ministries.

The true expression of love and trust in God is a generous heart. We should not be compelled to give simply because we are told to give a certain percentage. To give based on that understanding is to miss the glorious truth about redemption altogether. We ought to give simply because of what we have been given. We are moved to give when we realize the gift of life in Jesus Christ. I think one of the saddest moments in worship is when the offering plates are passed. I have often looked out and seen faces just cave into themselves when they had to part with their dollar.

Once again, giving is not about giving away something for the sake of duty. We should look at generous giving as an investment. Paul says to the Philippians, "Not that I seek the gift itself, but I seek for the profit which increases to your account" (4:17 NASB). Paul says to the Corinthians, "Each man should give what he has decided in his heart to give, not reluctantly or under compulsion, for God loves a cheerful giver" (2 Cor. 9:7 NIV). We should not look at giving as a matter of having to give and losing those extra precious dollars. We should look at giving as an investment in eternity. Paul tells Timothy, "Tell them to use their money to do good. They should be rich in good works and should give happily to those in need, always being ready to share with others whatever God has given them. By doing this they will be storing up real treasure for themselves in heaven—it is the only safe investment for eternity! And they will be living a fruitful Christian life down here as well" (1 Tim. 6:18-19 TLB).

Paul is also mindful of the truth of the Gospel. The gift that he received was not only a benefit to him but it was a fragrant aroma of sacrifice to God. He says, "But I have received everything in full and have an abundance; I am amply supplied, having received from Epaphroditus what you have sent, a fragrant aroma, an acceptable sacrifice, well-pleasing to God" (4:18 NASB).

Jesus one time spoke of the judgment and He said that the sheep would be placed on His right and the goats on His left (cf. Matt. 25:31-40). The ones on His right were rewarded with a heavenly reward. He explains why they were rewarded, "For I was hungry and you gave me something to eat, I was thirsty and you gave me something to drink, I was a stranger and you invited me in, I needed clothes and you clothed me, I was sick and you looked after me, I was in prison and you came to visit me (vs.35-36)." But the people were asking "When did we do these things?" and Jesus says, " . . . I tell you the truth, whatever you did for one of the least of these brothers of mine, you did for me" (vs.40).

Every act of kindness, of generosity, of sacrifice, every act of love we do for others is like doing it for Jesus. When we do it in the name of Jesus and for the sake of the Gospel it is like "a fragrant aroma, an acceptable sacrifice, well-pleasing to God." Several times in the Old Testament it says that when they sacrificed to the Lord it was like a soothing, or pleasing aroma. Neil Diamond once sang, *"I can still recall the smell of cookin in the hallways* (Neil Diamond, Brooklyn Roads, Velvet Gloves and Spit, 1968)." I know what he means. I remember those bar-b-ques when my dad would be flaming steaks on the grill. You could smell that flagrance for blocks.

I don't know how God smells the fragrant aroma of our generosity but I do know that He knows. Nothing escapes His notice. Do you remember the woman who gave the two mites? Other people were giving these elaborate gifts but this woman gave all that she had. Jesus takes notice. He says she truly gave because she gave all of what she had. You may think that God hasn't noticed that gift, that act of kindness, that moment of selfless sacrifice, but He has and He has banked it into your heavenly account. Jesus said, "Do not store up for yourselves treasures on earth . . . But store up for yourselves treasures in heaven." But then He says, "For where your treasure is, there your heart will be also" (Matt. 6:19-21 NIV).

You cannot invest in heaven with a selfish heart. You cannot make the claim that you are a Christian just because you attend a church or you abstain from certain practices. True Christianity begins in the heart and is expressed by living that life daily. I can do all things, you can do all things. Nothing is left to chance or selfish effort. We can do all things through Christ. That is the connection we all must have. We can do all things by the power of Jesus Christ. The power that gives us that ability is not self effort but resurrection power. And when you and I rest in that power we find true contentment.

# 23

# The Journey Of Promise
# Philippians 4:19

A promise is only as good as the character of the one making that promise. As I think about this, I think about the promise my parents made to my brothers and sisters and me. They didn't make this declaration out loud or put it on a piece of paper. They made this promise in their hearts. They made a promise to each other in their relationship and in their responsibilities. They made this promise that they would do everything they could to see that we had a place to live, food to eat, clothes to wear, an education to achieve and a character that would not disappoint.

They didn't have to spell it out for us, they just lived it. My dad worked hard for many years to provide the things necessary to keep the family alive. When times were tough my mom went to work for a while. But in all of their efforts the over arching purpose was not for self gratification but for the sole purpose of honoring that promise. I cannot think of a time when we didn't have anything to eat, or were out on the street or lacked the necessary clothing to go to school in. We didn't always have an abundance of things. My parents couldn't always afford a new car or a fancy house. But what they did have was this abundance of love in their hearts. Even to the day they died they kept on honoring that promise, to give to us.

This is Paul's final thought on the difference between a true believer and a card-carrying church member. He says, "And my God will supply all your needs according to His riches in glory in Christ Jesus" (Phil. 4:19 NASB). When we read this we often miss the importance of these few words. Paul always has in mind the God who showed mercy to him. He has never forgotten or even gotten over the Damascus road experience. For Paul, God was as real to him at this point in his life as he was when he first gave his life to Him.

Paul has given to the Philippians the doctrinal proof of a true believer and the practical examples of a true believer. But now he gives them a personal exposition of a true believer. He says, *"My God."* How often have we heard people make this statement of amazement or displeasure "My God!" Believers are equally guilty of using this phrase as a statement of displeasure or surprise. But Paul does not use this as a statement in that way. He uses it as an affirmation, *"My God."*

God is a personal friend. He is involved in this intimate relationship with Him. Paul doesn't see God as just some spiritual being somewhere out there in the cosmos. God is his God. It is the same way with my identification with my parents. They are my parents. Frank is "my" father and Belen is "my" mother. I know them because I have experienced them. I have been loved by them. I have been cared for by them. They are "my" parents. And when we look at God or consider God in our lives do we see Him as "MY GOD?"

I believe this is where we lose sight of who we are. There is a tendency to see God as some distant being aware of our activities but having no intimacy with us. I realize that many of us live with this theological concept of God. We have the information, this ability to discuss everything that is written about Him. We have the facts but do we have a heart to heart interaction with Him? Then again we also have the propensity to swing to the other side and think of all of this as just experience or emotion. We have no time or desire for understanding doctrines. We depend on an emotional experience. It is the feeling we are looking for.

While these two things are necessary they cannot exist without the other. Paul said, "For me to live is Christ and to die is gain." That was his emotional experience. But then he also says, "that I may know Him." This is his doctrinal experience. We need both. This is a unique fact that true believers need to understand. What Paul means by *"my God"* is that He can be personally experienced. God has the ability and the willingness to interact with His children much like my parents did with me. Let me be clear here. This knowledge comes only to those that are truly His children. I know many people say we are all God's children but the fact of the matter is we are not. While we may all be the creation of God we are not all the children of God. The Bible makes that very clear. The teachings of the Apostles make that very clear. John says in His Gospel, "But as many as received Him, to them He gave the right to become children of God" (John 1:12 NASB).

So when Paul says *"my God"* he is saying that he knows Him and has experienced Him. Paul is convinced of the inner workings of God in his life. He has seen where he was and where he is now. God has been involved every step of the way. He goes on to say that he not only has this knowledge and experience but he has also achieved a state of contentment with God. He says, "And my God will supply all your needs" (v.19). There was nothing lacking in his life. No matter what circumstance he was facing, rich or poor, hungry or fed, having or lacking, he always knew he would never be without because, "my God will supply." King David said, "I have been young, and now am old; Yet have I not seen the righteous forsaken, Nor his seed begging bread" (Psalms 37:25 ASV).

My parents never forced us to go and look for food. In a family of eleven it would have been easy to force us to go out to the street corners and beg for money to buy food. I see a lot of people out with their cardboard signs begging for money to buy food or gas. I am sure that a lot of these folks truly are in need of assistance, but there are a few that abuse the process. They have the ability to work but they refuse to do so. I have also seen parents send their children out to beg for money. I can honestly say that my parents did whatever it took to provide for us.

Paul tells these Christians at Philippi not to worry about tomorrow *"my God will supply."* Don't worry about what you are experiencing *"my God will supply."* Don't give up because you cannot see the light at the end of the tunnel *"my God will supply."* God's provisions are not always monetary or physical, they are also spiritual. Are you feeling the temptation to give up on God? Wait, *"my God will supply."* Are you in a financial situation and you can't see the light at the end of the tunnel? Wait, *"my God will supply."* Are you in a relationship that is going nowhere and you have prayed and agonized over this situation and just don't know what else to do? Wait, *"my God will supply."*

The wealth of God is endless. You and I have the privilege of having a portion of that wealth. What we do with it and how we use it really depends on what we believe about God and how we relate to Him. The Bible tells us that He owns the cattle on a thousand hills (Ps. 50:10). You and I cannot imagine the wealth of God. It is beyond our understanding. What we can know is that He will never leave His children destitute or begging for bread. So why is it that there are Christians who are poor wondering the streets, begging at churches or seem to have no purpose in life?

We often have this tendency to lead people to believe that when we give our hearts to Christ that everything is going to be perfect. We aren't going to be troubled by anything or need anything. That's the trouble with people who teach this prosperity doctrine. It is misleading and it is in direct conflict with the teachings of the Apostles. While God does not desire His children to be beggars, it is the individual themselves that sometimes brings this misery into their lives. God is not against riches. He never condemns wealth, but what He does not approve of is this love for wealth. We equate faithfulness or spirituality with how much wealth we have or have been "blessed" with. Listen, you can be a wealthy Christian and I see no problem with that. But what concerns me is how we get that wealth and the manner in which we use that wealth. Too many of these high profile preachers and teachers who claim to be a Christian flaunt their wealth. They are neither humble nor generous.

The promise here is not in getting from God what I want or desire. It is getting from God what I need. Paul says, "my God will supply all your needs." Here again this is where we get into trouble. We mistake a want for a need. Let's be truthful here, many of the needs we say we have are not needs at all. Sometimes we wind up in a bad situation simply because we let our wants dictate our decisions. When that happens we wind up on the side of the road broken down or just out of gas. This is true of the way we handle our money, our relationships and our lives. Some of us have this idea that God is some big dispensing machine. We go up to it, slide our church membership card in and punch up some numbered blessing. When we get what we want then we're good to go.

God does not work that way and Paul lets us know. He says God will supply all of our *needs*. Paul knew what it was to be in need and he tells us that in verses 11-12 of this last chapter. Yet, he had never experienced total destitution. In every situation God had met his need either by the Philippian church or other churches that supported him. God even provided opportunities for him to work. Let me just say one last thing here, God is under no obligation to do one thing for us. He meets or provides for our needs because we are His children. My mom and dad were not obligated to help me as I got older. They helped me because they loved me. And God gives simply because He loves.

Paul tells the believers that God is a giver. He gives generously and consistently. He says, "And my God will supply all your needs according to His riches." Here is a picture of God's generosity. God gives us more than a token gift. God gives in such a way that it satisfies. The word **"supply"** here means to **"make full"** or **"to complete."** You and I can never out give God. That is what Paul is telling these Christians. They had given to Paul from their heart. They made great sacrifices so that he could continue to minister, and therefore God blesses them beyond all measure. God doesn't measure out his blessings, He pours them out.

Notice one final thought here, something I have tried to stress throughout this book. Paul says that these riches that are given to the Christian are found only in one place and that is in Jesus Christ. What we may think of as having value is not more valuable than the relationship that we have in Christ. To be in Christ is to be fully cared for and guarded. As believers we have an inheritance in Jesus, " . . . in whom are hidden all the treasures of wisdom and knowledge" (Col. 2:3 NASB). As believers we have an inheritance with Jesus, " . . . and if children, then heirs—heirs of God and joint heirs with Christ" (Rom. 8:17 NKJV). As believers we have an inheritance through Jesus, "And if you belong to Christ, then you are Abraham's descendants, heirs according to promise, according to His riches in glory in Christ Jesus" (Gal. 3:29 NASB).

What a wonderful thing to know that God can be "my God." God is my Father who can hear me when I need His help. David said, "In my distress I called upon the Lord, and cried to my God for help; He heard my voice out of His temple, And my cry for help before Him came into His ears" (Ps. 18:6 NASB). But God is not only a source of comfort and protection, but someone in whom we can have pride in. David said again, "Then I will praise you with music on the harp, because you are faithful to your promises, O my God. I will sing praises to you with a lyre, O Holy One of Israel" (Ps. 71:22 NLT).

To Paul, God was very personal. He tells the Philippians at the beginning, "I thank my God in all my remembrance of you" (1.3). He has known Him, served Him and experienced Him. He knew about His love and concern for Him. In Paul's life he could truly say he lacked nothing. He knew contentment because of the promise of God, to supply his every need. This journey to joy is one in where we are firmly grounded in God's faithfulness to His children, "And my God will supply all your needs according to His riches in glory in Christ Jesus."

# 24

# Conclusion
# Philippians 4:20-23

We have come through one of the most exciting journeys thus far, the journey to joy. I am always amazed at how God moves in our lives as we continue to grow in Him and learn about Him. No journey is without hardship or uncertainty. But the journey of the Christian life is not one in which we should be caught off guard. We should know who we are and more importantly we should know whose we are. We are the children of God. That means every believer is a part of the family of God. And nothing is as valuable as family. I don't care how selfish we can be at times, nothing can ever change the fact that we are a family and that God is our Heavenly Father.

It didn't matter how much I disagreed with my mom and dad. It didn't matter how much or how often I fought with my brothers and sisters. Nothing could ever change the fact that they were my family and that my mom and dad would always be my parents. Paul says to the Christians in Rome, "Who, then, can separate us from the love of Christ? Can trouble do it, or hardship or persecution or hunger or poverty or danger or death? . . . For I am certain that nothing can separate us from his love . . . there is nothing in all creation that will ever be able to separate us from the love of God which is ours through Christ Jesus our Lord" (Rom. 8:35-39 TEV).

The Apostle John, in writing to these believers, wanted to make absolutely certain that they knew who they were and whose they were.

He says, "See how great a love the Father has bestowed on us, that we would be called children of God; and such we are . . . Beloved, now we are children of God, and it has not appeared as yet what we will be. We know that when He appears, we will be like Him, because we will see Him just as He is . . . By this the children of God and the children of the devil are obvious: anyone who does not practice righteousness is not of God, nor the one who does not love his brother" (1 John 3:1-2 & 10 NASB).

There is a great distinction between a believer, and one who claims to be but is not. A Christian not only lives the life of a believer but also recognizes that all believers are in a family. We are one in Christ. It doesn't matter what title we may place on ourselves. If we have trusted in Jesus Christ as our Lord and Savior, hold to the truths of Holy Scripture as the Apostles directed us, then we are children of God. We are a family.

This is where Paul draws one final truth and hope. He says in the concluding verses of this fourth chapter, "Now to our God and Father be the glory forever and ever. Amen. Greet every saint in Christ Jesus. The brethren who are with me greet you. All the saints greet you, especially those of Caesar's household. The grace of the Lord Jesus Christ be with your spirit" (Phil. 4:20-23 NASB).

This is about being in the family of God. He says "Now to our God and Father be the glory forever and ever." We have to know that God is our Father and we must be certain that He has our best interest at heart. Paul says again, "I am convinced that God who began a good work . . . will complete it." A father who loves his children will never send them out into the world without any means of protection and provision. A good father will not only seek to protect his children, provide for them but he will also lead by instruction and illustration. That is what my parents tried to achieve with all of us. Because of that, we have great respect for them. We did not always understand the process anymore than our own children did, but they stayed the course. And as I grow older and look back, I can see all that they tried to accomplish. I have come to respect them all the more.

That is what Paul means when he says, "Now to our God and Father be the glory forever and ever." He looked back and saw the workings of God in his life and he reminded the Philippian Christians of the same thing. When we know and have experienced God working in our lives, experienced his protection and provisions all along this journey, we show our love to Him by glorifying Him. Another way of saying it is that we have a reverence or respect for Him. He is my God and He is your God. He is our Father.

Then Paul goes on to say that we should, "Greet every saint in Christ Jesus." The word *"greet"* carries the idea of *"welcoming another."* This statement carries the idea of brotherly affection. Long lasting families remain that way because of brotherly affection. This is not something superficial. In the church today we sometimes have the pretense of affection but in all actuality have no real deep concerns for one another. I have been in ministry long enough to know that we all have our petty differences, that cause a church to waver or become stagnate. I am not saying we have to all think alike or do everything one way. We are all different, but the teaching here is that we are to be " . . . of the same mind, maintaining the same love, united in spirit, intent on one purpose (2:2). We can disagree in the non-essentials but in the essentials we must be united.

Paul says to the Corinthians, "I appeal to you, dear brothers and sisters, by the authority of our Lord Jesus Christ, to live in harmony with each other. Let there be no divisions in the church. Rather, be of one mind, united in thought and purpose" (1 Cor. 1:10 NLT). To the Christians in Rome Paul says, "Live in harmony with each other. Don't be too proud to enjoy the company of ordinary people. And don't think you know it all!" (Rom. 12:16 NLT). And then once again to these Philippian Christians he says, "Make my joy complete by being of the same mind, maintaining the same love, united in spirit, intent on one purpose" (Phil. 2:2 NASB).

Finally he says, "The brethren who are with me greet you. All the saints greet you, especially those of Caesar's household" (vs. 21-22). Notice the progression here. Unity begins with us personally when we are right with God our Father and then it proceeds to our inner circle and then finally to the outer circle. True believers are connected to each other no matter where we are or what we do. We are connected by the blood of Jesus Christ. To be a true believer has nothing, absolutely nothing, to do with denominational preferences. It is not a Baptist thing or a Methodist thing or a Catholic thing. We can be anything we want to be and still never make it into heaven. That has been the problem, in my mind, with the church today. Many falsely believe that you have to be of this or that denomination. If not, then you are not a Christian.

Listen, Christianity is not a denomination! It is a way of life. The New Testament believers were not concerned about being of this church or that church. They were concerned about the Christian life and all of their teachings reflected that concern. That is why we must always search the Scriptures for the true way of the Christian life. Once again Paul emphasizes this truth when he says, "The grace of the Lord Jesus Christ be with your spirit" (v.23). This is a statement that has purpose as Paul closes this letter. It is not some afterthought. Paul never uses this statement causally. He has a reason for using it.

Considering all that Paul has told us about the Christian life, he is mindful once again to reiterate the differences between living the a *good life* and living the *Christian life*. He says, "The grace of the Lord Jesus Christ." This is where it begins, with grace. Now grace, according to the scholars, is that *"unmerited favor, unearned and undeserved."* Christians are not better people they are *changed people*. The Bible tells us that before we became children of God we were enemies of God. Paul tells us, "for all have sinned and fall short of the glory of God." In the previous verses of this same chapter Paul says, "What then? Are we better than they? Not at all; for we have already charged that both Jews and Greeks are all under sin; as it is written, 'There is none righteous, not even one'" (Rom. 3:23; 3:9-10 NASB). When we are born into this world we are born sinners. None of us can escape that fact. Paul tells the Romans, "For the sin of this one man, Adam, brought death to many" (Rom. 5:15 NLT). All have sinned, that is Paul's message to every one of us. For Christians to think they are better than someone else is to misunderstand the Scriptures.

There is nothing external that anyone of us can do to become a Christian. We can pray until our knees are black and blue. We can give until we have nothing else to give. We can serve until we cannot serve anymore. We can go to church until the end of time and yet none of these things will give us eternal life. We are sinners and sin cannot enter the Kingdom of God. Paul tells us, "we were utterly helpless" (Rom. 5:6 NLT). So what's the secret? How can we have eternal life if none of these things can give it to us? GRACE! We need God's grace. God's grace is this, **God Reaching And Christ Entering**.

God saw our need long before we were born. He reached out to us even when we didn't think we needed Him. He loved us when we were not the most lovable of people. He took that first step when we felt we already knew the right direction. John tells us that God so loved the world (John. 3:16). That is God reaching to us long before we even knew He cared. Paul tells us that God demonstrated that love while we were yet sinners (Romans 5:8). He didn't wait until we cleaned up our act or changed our ways. He took the first step and demonstrated that love. But the choice is still ours to make. The offer of grace is there but if we do not accept it we cannot enter the kingdom of heaven. We must confess our need and accept the gift (Romans 10:9-10). You and I must take that step of faith and accept Jesus. Paul tells the Ephesians "God saved you by his grace when you believed" (Eph.2:8 NLT). You have to have faith. The writer of Proverbs says, "Trust in the Lord with all your heart and do not lean on your own understanding." (Prov. 3:5 NASB).

Paul goes on to say, "And you can't take credit for this; it is a gift from God. Salvation is not a reward for the good things we have done, so none of us can boast about it" (Eph. 2:9 NLT). You and I cannot come to Jesus thinking that we are special people. We can't have the attitude that Jesus really got something when He got us. Paul has already told us to exhibit humility in our lives. James tells the believers, "Humble yourselves before the Lord, and he will lift you up" (James 4:10 NIV). Peter says basically the same thing, "Humble yourselves, therefore, under God's mighty hand, that he may lift you up in due time" (1 Pet. 5:6 NIV).

To be a believer is not just to change a few things here and there to become a better person. To be a true believer is to become a new creation, and that only happens when God begins His good work in you. The rest of Paul's statement to the Ephesians says this, "For we are God's masterpiece. He has created us anew in Christ Jesus, so we can do the good things he planned for us long ago" (Eph. 2:10 NLT). We are a work in progress. We are becoming God's masterpiece if we allow Him to work in our lives. We need God's grace to be called the true believers. This life cannot begin and end with us. It must begin and end in Jesus Christ. There are a variety of denominations that will teach that there are other means to heaven. But as the Word of God says plainly, "Before every man there lies a wide and pleasant road he thinks is right, but it ends in death" (Prov. 16:25 TLB).

Then Paul finishes his statement with this phrase, "The grace of the Lord Jesus Christ **be with your spirit**." What does he mean here? It means that if we are truly God's children we are connected to God through our spirit. We cannot have this connection without the grace of the Lord Jesus Christ. Grace allows our spirit to enjoy fellowship with God. This is the thing that is raised in the likeness of His resurrection. Fellowship with God cannot be obtained by external activities. This is why it is so important to be aware that God is working in our lives. It is that living spirit within us that gives credibility to that fact.

That is the final thought Paul wants to impress on these believers. If they have a right spirit about them, then whatever may be taking place in their lives, they will be able to rise above it. That is where Paul was. He was in prison and his life was in the hands of his captors. In this letter we have seen how he has come to the place in his life where he knows, he is convinced that God will not fail him nor forsake him. For Paul could truly say, "For me to live is Christ, and to die is gain."

As believers we need to know that God's grace watches over us. No matter where we are in this journey, God's grace will never fail us. Joy is not the absence of trouble or living a life of endurance. We cannot implement joy into our lives by doing certain things or by holding onto certain truths. Joy is knowing that God has begun a good work in us and that He does not intend on giving up. As a Christian you may have failed in your walk with God, but He has not given up on you. You may have had a bad relationship that ended in separation and you feel like God is never going to use you again. Friend, God has not given up on you. You may have made bad decisions with your wealth, your family or your integrity. Listen, the Bible tells us, "You, LORD, will not forsake your people, nor abandon your very own" (Ps. 94:14 NAB).

Our spirit is connected to God through His grace, but we are also connected to each other by this spirit. We are a true family if we have been saved by God's grace. Jesus didn't just die for one particular people. The Bible tells us that His death was "to bring together and unite all the children of God scattered around the world" (John 11:52 NLT). One day God will bring all believers together and it will not be by denominations. I truly believe that there won't be any Baptists, Brethren, Methodists, Catholics or any other denomination in heaven. I do believe that only the **Children of God** will be there.

I also believe that we won't live in separate housing either. Jesus tell us that, "In my Father's house are many rooms" (John 14:2 NIV). I know that there have been songs written about the mansions up above, but in my opinion they are wrong. In God's house, in my Father and your Father's house there are many rooms. Families are meant to live together, not apart. Here on earth, as Christians, we have been slow to understand the uniqueness of our relationship as Christians. We are a family.

We have journeyed far together and it is my hope and prayer that you will know true joy as God leads you in His direction. Never give up on yourself. Never lose sight of who you are. Never let anyone tell you you're worthless. God loves you so much that He willingly gave you what was most precious to Him, His Son. There is no greater gift than Jesus Christ. And you can give no greater gift to the Father of lights than your undying devotion to Him.

> "You will be like a beautiful crown in the Lord's hand,
> like a king's crown in your God's hand . . .
> His people will be called the Holy People,
> the Saved People of the Lord,
> and Jerusalem will be called the City God Wants,
> the City God Has Not Rejected."
> Isaiah 62:3&12 (NCV)

# Works Consulted

Berry, George R. *Parallel New Testament in Greek and English*. Grand Rapids: Zondervan Publishing House, 1897.

Boice, James M. *Philippians*. 1 vol. 2nd ed. Grand Rapids: Baker Books, 2000.

Boice, James M. *Romans 5-8*. Vol. 2. 4th ed. Grand Rapids: Baker Book House, 2000. 4 vols.

Bromiley, Geoffrey W. *Theological Dictionary Of The New Testament*. 1 vol. 2nd ed. Grand Rapids: William B. Eerdmans Publishing Company, 1988.

Bruce, F.F. *The Gospel of John*. 1 vol 2nd ed. Grand Rapids: William B. Eerdmans Publishing Company, 1989.

MacArthur, John F. "The Distinctive Qualities of the True Christian." 2009. 4 July 2009 <http://www.gty.org/Resources/Sermons/50-27, 50-28, 50-29>.

MacArthur, John F. *The MacArthur New Testament Commentary Matthew 1-7*. Vol. 1. Chicago: Moody Press, 1985. 4 vols.

Lloyd-Jones, D. Martyn. *The Life of Joy*. 1 vol. 2nd ed. Grand Rapids: Baker Book House, 1993.

Lloyd-Jones, D. Martyn. *The Life of Peace*. 1 vol. 2nd ed. Grand Rapids: Baker Book House, 1992.

Marshall D.Litt, Alfred. *The Interlinear Greek—English New Testament*. 1 vol. 2nd ed. Grand Rapids: Zondervan Publishing House, 1975.

Moule D.D, Handley C G. *Philippian Studies*. 1 vol. 2nd ed. London: Pickering and Inglis, n.d.

Whitelaw, Rev. Thomas. *The Gospel of St. John, An Exposition, Exegetical and Homiletical*. 1 vol. Fincastle, VA: Scripture Truth Book Company, n.d.

Edwards Brothers Malloy
Oxnard, CA USA
May 26, 2015